# maverick MANAGEMENT

## Also by John W. Hartman

*Selling Your Business: How to Make the Best Deal*

*Second Thoughts*

*Add/More Second Thoughts*

*Return of Second Thoughts*

# maverick MANAGEMENT

## An Unconventional Guide to Success

by John W. Hartman

with Harvey Mackay, John Templeton
Cathleen Black, Butch Granville,
William Phillips, Bob Galvin,
Ren McPherson, Bill Ruder,
Geoff Simmonds, Jack Linkletter,
Bo Callaway . . . and others

CORMORANT PRESS
PHILADELPHIA

**_CORMORANT PRESS, LTD._**
_842 South Second Street, Suite 351_
_Philadelphia, PA 19147_
_(215) 922-3009_



First Edition 1998
Printed and bound in the United States of America

Library of Congress Cataloging-in-Publication Data.
Hartman, John W. and contributors
John W. Hartman and contributors—
First Cormorant Press ed.
Includes index
ISBN: 1-885884-03-6
Library of Congress Catalog Card Number: 97-68808

Editorial Coordinator: Carolyn Cioffi
Index: Genevieve Kedziera
Dust Jacket & Book Design: Doreen Naughton/Cormorant Design

*To my patient wife,*
*who reads and edits*
*every loving word*

# PREFACE

Those who worship the conventional wisdoms and aspire always to be politically correct will probably be uncomfortable with parts of this book.

And then there are those who enjoy looking at many things just a little differently, occasionally finding solutions by turning their approaches upside-down, have no need to necessarily follow the pack, are just as content following their own paths.

They are really not "anti-establishment" or anti-anything. Rather, they prefer perhaps to look at things, address problems or challenges, maybe just five percent differently than the conventional route.

For most things they have a healthy constructive skepticism. But they are not in any way cynics. Indeed they are optimistic, pragmatic, idealist. And these words are not oxymoronic.

Webster's defines "unconventional" as: "not bound by or in accordance with convention: being out of the ordinary."

The dictionary definition of "maverick" includes: "a range animal that is not following his mother: sets an independent course." Apparently the term originated in 1870 about Samuel A. Maverick, a Texan who did not brand his calves.

Advertising legend David Ogilvy, in his *Confessions of An Advertising Man*, notes: "After 14 years in the business, I came to the conclusion that the top man has one principal responsibility: to provide an atmosphere in which creative mavericks can do useful work."

This book is a collection of unconventional and maverick personal experiences, as reflected in columns I wrote over a number of years. It is supplemented by contributions from fellow mavericks. Good reading.

# About The Author

John W. Hartman served as Chief Executive Officer of Bill Communications, Inc. for over thirty years. During that time, he gradually became the publishing firm's principal stockholder. Under Hartman's direction, Bill Communications established itself as a model for participative, decentralized management. Several of his unconventional innovations, such as "Bottoms Up Management," remain to this day as case studies in educational institutions such as Harvard's business school.

As a publisher of trade magazines, Hartman was no stranger to the written word. His witty and prescient writings appeared regularly in a number of Bill Communications publications, including *Sales and Marketing Management Magazine*. He continues currently as a contributing columnist for *Business Marketing, Advertising Age, The Free Press* (Florida Keys), *Across The Board* (The Conference Board), *The Shoreline Press*, and various trade and business magazines. He has authored the following books: *Selling Your Business: How to Make the Best Deal; Second Thoughts; ADD/MORE Second Thoughts;* and *Return of Second Thoughts.*

Hartman has served as International President of the Young Presidents Organization (YPO) and as Forum Chairman and board member of the Chief Executives Organization. He founded the Executive Council of The Conference Board and is a member of the World Presidents Council.

In January of 1989, Hartman finalized the sale of Bill Communications for a price in the area of $100 million. He and his wife, Kelly, live in Ocean Reef, Florida.

# About the Contributors

**Joseph Avenick**

Author, literary agent, business consultant. Former sports columnist for *Philadelphia Inquirer*. Chief researcher for author James A. Michener.

**Cathleen P. Black**

Successes in both the magazine and newspaper fields include Associate Publisher of *Ms.,* Publisher of *New York* and *USA Today,* and President and CEO of the American Newspaper Publisher's Association. Currently President of Hearst Magazines. A Chicago native, she was graduated from Washington, D. C.'s Trinity College.

**Howard "Bo" Callaway**

Chairman of Callaway Gardens and Crested Butte, Inc. West Point graduate. Korea army service. Former Secretary of Army. Past international president, Young Presidents' Organization and World Presidents' Organization. Lives in Pine Mountain, Georgia.

**Jim Dickie II**

President of Crown Equipment, a privately held worldwide manufacturer of forklifts and material handling equipment. Former international president of the Young Presidents' Organization. Graduate of Culver and Trinity University. Lives in Bremen, Ohio.

**Walter Forbes**

Chairman and CEO, C.U.C. International. Northwestern and Harvard Business Schools. Resides in New Canaan, Connecticut.

**Don Gabbert**

Retired CEO of Gabbert Furniture and Gabbert Appliances. Formerly with University of Minnesota and Fuller Brush

Company. Philanthropist. Resides at Ocean Reef Club, Florida and Minneapolis.

**Bob Galvin**

Chairman and CEO of Motorola during its most formative years, 1959-1990. Motorola was the first large company to win the Malcolm Baldridge Quality Awards, in 1988. Attended Notre Dame and the University of Chicago. Resides at Barrington, Illinois.

**Alan Goldstein**

Chairman and CEO of Business Methods, Inc. Past Chairman, Ocean Reef Club. Syracuse University. Lives at Ocean Reef Club, Florida and Winter Harbor, Maine.

**Maurice "Butch" Granville**

Chairman and CEO of Texaco, Inc., 1972-1980. Chairman of American Petroleum Institute, 1976-77. Director, Federal Reserve Bank of New York, 1972-79. Numerous boards. Graduate of University of Texas and MIT. Residences: Ocean Reef Club, Florida and Rockport, Maine.

**Leo Greenland**

Founded, in 1958, and was CEO of Smith/Greenland advertising agency. Current president of the Friar's Club Foundation. Resides in New York City.

**Don J. Hindman**

Chairman and CEO of Clark Foodservice, Inc., one of the largest food distributor services in the U.S. A World War II Air Force veteran. Born in Kansas, raised in West Virginia and a graduate of the University of Indiana, he now lives in Oak Brook, Illinois and Ocean Reef Club, Florida.

**Joseph Klock**

Founded Klock Realtors, then merged it with Coldwell Banker in 1983. Past president of Brokers Managers Council, National Association of Realtors. Dean of Coldwell Banker

University, public speaker, newspaper columnist. Lives in Key Largo, Florida.

**Jack Linkletter**
President of Linkletter Enterprises (network television series, commercial and industrial real estate, and investment management). Past international president of Young Presidents' Organization. Lecturer, consultant.

**Harvey B. Mackay**
Chairman and CEO, Mackay Envelope Company. Best-selling business book author of *Swim with the Sharks* and other books. University of Minnesota. Lives in Excelsior, Minnesota.

**Ren McPherson**
Past Chairman and CEO of Dana Corporation. Former Dean of Stanford School of Business. Most listed index references in Peters and Waterman's *In Search of Excellence*. Resided at Ocean Reef Club, Florida and Toledo, Ohio. Died in 1995.

**William Phillips**
Retired Chairman and CEO of Ogilvy & Mather agency. Chairman of Outward Bound. Says, "learned at some good schools," including Cornell. U.S. Navy, Korea. Motto: "You do what you want, you are what you do."

**William Ryan**
President and CEO of the heavy and highway construction companies, Ryan, Inc. University of Wisconsin. World War II U.S. Army. Resides in Janesville, Wisconsin and Deerfield Beach, Florida.

**Bill Ruder**
Founded Ruder & Finn, one of the largest public relations firms in the world, in 1948. Former U.S. Assistant Secretary of Commerce. Presently head of Ruder Incorporated. Resides in New York City.

**Herman Shepherd**

Chairman of Sabin Foundation. Former Chairman, Armstrong Pharmaceuticals. Cornell University. Resides in New Canaan, Connecticut.

**Geoff Simmonds**

Built a small aerospace company into $200 million sales, went public, sold it to Hercules, Inc. Born in the United Kingdom, educated at the Harrow School and Magdalene, Cambridge. Now resides in Fort Lauderdale where he heads a medical equipment company.

**Roger Sonnabend**

Chairman and CEO, Sonesta International Hotel Corporation. Past international president of Young Presidents' Organization. Resides at Key Biscayne, Florida and Boston.

**Sir John Templeton**

Legendary investor and founder of Templeton Investment Funds. Under his stewardship, an original Templeton Growth Fund investment of $10,000 grew to over $3 million 37 years later. Now a philanthropist who gifts $30 million annually for Progress in Religion. Attended Yale and Oxford as a Rhodes scholar. Resides at Lyford Cay, the Bahamas.

**Rick VanGrouw**

Now an on-line editor at the Canton (Ohio) Repository. For over six years he was managing editor of three weekly newspapers in the Florida Keys. He was graduated from Indiana's Valparaiso University.

**Charles West**

Chairman Emeritus of the building material chain, West Enterprises. Graduated from Emory University. U.S. Navy 1942-45. Lives in Atlanta, Georgia.

**David Whitney**

His eclectic career ranges from an outdoor columnist for *Florida Times Union* to Associated Press writer and editor, to publisher/founder of weekly Florida Keys newspapers. Author of three books and three-time nominee for the Pulitzer Prize. Home is Pigeon Key, Florida Keys.

**Brian Wolfson**

CEO of Anglo-Nordic Holdings. Past international president of Young Presidents' Organization. Enjoyed an international career in senior management positions, both in public and private sectors involving startup situations in over 30 countries. Major commitment and involvement in training, both in-house and as a leader of government task force. Headquarters and residence: London, England.

# CONTENTS

## PART THREE: PLANNING



## PART FOUR: SALES AND MARKETING



## PART FIVE: INVESTING AND WALL STREET

# INTRODUCTION

Conventional managers go by the book. Unconventional Managers read the book and then discard it. Then they write their own.

Conventional managers relish the power lunch. Unconventional Managers skip lunch. They use the time to prepare for the afternoon "kill."

Conventional managers impose strict guidelines for employee salary levels. Unconventional Managers, instead, challenge employees with: "What's the most that someone can make?"

Conventional managers seek the guidance of experts. Unconventional Managers listen to the experts, yes, but then to themselves and to their employees in the trenches—and most of all to their customers.

Why Unconventional Management?

Answer it thusly: Why Profits? Why Success?

It is unlikely that conventional management will spur the next soaring trend—and just as unlikely that traditional techniques will ever unearth innovative change.

**Extra Edges of Excellence**

Unconventional Managers can not only bring their businesses to new exhilarating heights but they can also keep their firms alive when times are toughest. The secret lies in finding those Extra Edges of Excellence—be they in people or in procedures.

Being an Unconventional Manager is not something we can zap on-and-off from our easy chairs like a VCR remote. We have to work at it constantly. Being unconventional is a 24-hour-a-day job.

Descriptions similar to the Extra Edges of Excellence—with the same bottom line—include Going The Extra Mile; and noting the difference between a baseball player who hits for a .290 average versus the player who bats at the Hall of Fame pace of .300 (the variation in number of hits amounts to just one per month over the course of a season, yet the difference in their salaries can be astronomical).

The difference of only one vote admitted Texas to the union, elected Jefferson president, made France a republic, and put the ruling house of England on the throne.

Despite these truths, the most experienced of us often let ourselves get stereotyped as managers and salespeople with routine tactics—the same cut-and-dried strategies that our competitor staffs are showering upon our mutual prospects. We don't have to be spectacularly different from our competitors, but with only five percent more time, five percent more think-through, there are a variety of little ways—Extra Edges—in which we can so easily differentiate ourselves—and our products.

As non-descript as some Extra Edges may first appear, they can, thanks to our perseverance, give us a surprisingly outstanding Different-From-The-Others image in the eyes of our prospects.

This leads to the next point. In order to find and exploit these Extra Edges, the Unconventional Manager must first have maverick ideas in place in the hierarchy of his firm. Most fish will bite at worms, yes. But others like to nibble at corn and bread crusts. Still others are raised on food pellets. So, instead of playing CYA games, the Unconventional Manager would rather cover all bases.

A great place for an unconventional start-up is with group dynamics. If we really desire a valuable reply when asking our managers and co-workers "What Do You Think?" we have to cut out those idea-stifling, conventional meetings. You know the kind, where monotone bean counters put everybody to sleep with their opening remarks on P&L, ROI, SG&A, and ZZZZ.

Next, we can effect a bottoms-up management structure, where no final word or directive is ever sent straight down the line. Give a mid-level employee a chance to conceive the right managerial moves—through participative planning. Participation at every level boosts the production of energetic ideas. And before too long, after getting all of this advice from the "bottom," you'll look around and find you have a thinner corporate staff. Yes, this is a threat to you if you are middle-staff management; but it's new opportunity if you are a middle line manager.

Avoid those deep ruts and restrictive grooves. Promise yourself and your fellow employees that you'll never stagnate at a self-imposed comfort level. With this in mind, one of your boldest moves would be to kick your best manager out of the office for awhile. Have him take an annual three-week sabbatical and talk to people on the outside. Maybe he'll learn about your customers. Forget the peddling of widgets. Sell some solutions instead.

Want to inspire loyalty? Reap the benefits of long-term employee allegiance?

Sell a piece of the rock to your employees. Bonuses and equity positions should go much deeper on your organizational chart. Heed a warning though: if you've been an Unconventional Manager for any length of time, you may not have a chart.

Dump those "Personnel" and "Human Resources" department labels. The trends that have a future are lurking, no doubt, in the brain waves at your People Office.

Encourage mistakes. Knowledge comes from trial-and-error, as do profits. Watch as the Unconventional Manager becomes so ingrained in your persona that maverick manipulations take over your leisure life as well.

Conventional managers only play golf at the club on Saturday morning. Unconventional Managers drag co-workers along on Wednesday morning to try the public course on the other side of the tracks. Conventional managers listen to their brokers and buy blue chip stocks with high yields. Unconventional Managers listen to their assistants, the ones who respond to “What Do You Think?” with a research report on weather patterns favoring grapefruit futures.

Conventional managers always take the home team when betting on pro football games, giving points; and they’ll always bet the favorites when they go to the races. Unconventional Managers know the difference between a risk and a gamble. Only Unconventional Managers will bet on 20-1 long shots to beat those favorites.

But at that price, they can afford to be wrong.

# PART ONE

# People & Resources

## Don't Let Our Best Progeny Get Sucked Into Management Consulting

*"MBAs and Their Prospects In Firms"*

(Excerpt from report to Duke University's Fuqua Graduate School of Business Board of Visitors by Executive Director of Hartman Center, Professor Preston C. Bottger, Nov. 1, 1995.)

*A telling example occurred at the beginning of Summer, 1995, which illustrates some of the challenges in placing our students with mid-sized firms.*

*A high-growth firm ($80 million in sales) based in St. Louis, MO, took two Fuqua MBAs as interns for Summer, 1994. The firm's president then tried to hire one of the students to join the firm on graduation.*

*In negotiations extending from September, 1994 to May, 1995, the firm stretched itself (in terms of internal equity with existing managers, etc.) to offer the student $65,000 to start. The student ended up joining a consulting firm starting at $75,000 with a $15,000 starting bonus.*

*As the president explained to me: He understands and accepts completely the student's decision and motivation, and the firm will try again with one of our students, but he did point out the difficulties that a mid-sized firm faces, even though highly motivated to hire one of our students.*

Look! Some of my best friends are management consultants. I golf, fish and tennis with some. Marvin Bowers, the spark and fountainhead of modern day McKinsey once even *asked me*, of all things, for advice on he and his wife's secret desire to start up and publish a new magazine. *(I advised "no," and years later Marvin said it was good advice.)*

McKinsey, Booz-Allen-Hamilton and others were helpful during my early business career. Sometimes a little off the mark, fuzzy, irrelevant . . . but more often constructive and useful, up to a point.

And that's the point. When it finally comes to *executing* their advice, all too often with consultants there are shortfalls. Theory is one thing; implementation is another. One alternative is to woo away one of the consultant's bright, young MBAers. But, trying then to integrate them into existing line operations is too often discouraging.

Sometimes it did work. Quite a few of my contemporary business executive friends did come from management consultant backgrounds. Generalizing, however, the shorter time they spent in the parasitical *(by definition)* consulting business before joining a "real business," the more successful they were. Even here they tended to shift around a lot, more "movers" than "shakers."

Why this coincidence of averageness with those who stayed too long in consulting before facing the real world? I suggest that after, say, five years of often generalized, abstract, presumptive, non-line consulting, they are perceived by the line in businesses as too spoiled for real leadership. After five years their B-School "computer smarts" have been wrung out of them, and are replaceable at lower costs in this regard. They become unpromoteable.

There's no argument that an emerging MBAer can start our making more dollars signing on with a management consultant firm. But check those crossing trend lines beginning five years out with those fellow graduates who started out a little lower when they instead chose to enter real businesses.

Even the former most mighty IBM who recruited and was perceived as kind of a management consulting company—and routinely scaled opening offers 10 percent above anybody else—is reviewing its past practices.

Advice to emerging MBAers: Look for the 10-20-30-year haul, not just the next five years.

*—November 1995*

## Be Sure Your Consultants Don't Just Make You Feel Good

"John, so far you're the least informed of our investment partners in our new business venture . . . let our president fully and thoroughly catch you up with events," cautioned Dick Carter. I had invested in his Evercolor, the new company with the revolutionary new sharper film processing that will never fade for generations.

"No, Dick," I replied. "I decline that offer of information. Rather, I believe my experience is that I can best serve you and others in the company by not becoming too professionally knowledgeable . . . ."

For 60 years Carter has been an upscale amateur photo-maven technically knowledgeable at least on a par with the best of the professionals. Me? Only recently did I venture beyond my Polaroid into the multi-alternative world of a sophisticated Nikon 8008. And, even to this day, I remain the camera-insecure type who still hasn't read the entire owner's manual. (I cop out saying maybe it's un-American to read all of the instructions.)

Now, all of my fellow business investors in Evercolor are almost as professionally camera-knowledgeable as Carter. Some of them can and do answer the photography questions before they've been asked—or even thought of. While I wallow behind in knowledgeability, all of their input is very useful to our company. After all, Evercolor is the next Dick Tracy Radio-Wristwatch in the field of digital imaging photography.

However, there's a key potential contribution to be made by readers no more technically hip than me. Non-specialists in your business can help keep you on top, I found out 45 years ago. After clawing our way to our media properties being number one—or contending with an entirely internal board of directors—and to keep the leading edge I enlisted two additional outside directors.

They couldn't have been more different . . . and uniquely valuable. J. Warren McClure, former head of *Burlington Free Press*, and second largest individual stockholder of Gannett Publishing, was very media knowledgeable. He often empathized and knew "the answers" of our six internal directors as well as they did.

The other outside director, the late Dillard Munford, was a maverick choice (lucky, it turned out). Although head of a New York Sock Exchange company, Munford—my friend of 30 years—liked to profess he knew nothing about media and publishing. But Munford did know people, consumer reactions—and the questions to ask.

The practice at our periodic board meetings was to rotate among our 13 divisional managers the challenge of presenting their progress and plans for the varying industries they served: food, restaurants, plastics, rubber, chemicals, travel, incentives, conferences, sales and marketing, home furnishings, automotive.

Outside director McClure, of course, knew media publishing, but it was impossible for he or Munford to be pros in all of our varied fields. So they played a variation of "Good Cop, Bad Cop." McClure would be professionally sympathetic to publishers' presentations, but a smiling Southern gentleman, Munford, was the maverick. Disarmingly scratching his head, offering a lame joke, apologizing for a "dumb question," Munford would say:

"Hey, I realize I don't know your business . . . but help me understand . . . . Why don't you . . . ? Why did you . . . ? Have you thought of . . . ?"

Several interesting things resulted. The editors, unable to anticipate the maverick questioning, took every presentation seriously and re-examined their previous assumptions, often altering them as a result. And, often a question from the "unknowledgeable" Munford would trigger an entirely different unanticipated perspective.

The value of the "uninformed" consultant continues to remind me that your typical prospective customer rarely knows as much—or cares about—your product as you do. A "hair-shirt" consultant can pay big dividends.

*—April 1994*

## Kick Your Best Manager Out Of The Office

Huh? Yup! Kick `em out. California-based Apple Computer, Inc. made news when it announced that its CEO would be on a six-week sabbatical. John Sculley, lauded in the press as a "heralded marketer who came to a troubled Apple after a successful presidency at Pepsi," practiced what company policy preached to all employees after five years of employment.

Management style watchers know that new trends and techniques often originate in kinky California and then seep back eastward through heartland America, tangenting at times to innovative Japan. (Generally, there's still a five to fifteen-year lag in European adoption.)

Sculley's six weeks of "gone fishing" (except for a few key meetings) followed a return to record sales and income for Apple, at the time. Predictably, Wall Street savants reinforced their record of being the last to know what's really happening in business: Sculley's sabbatical announcement drove down the stock one-and-one-half points. But, as Sculley said, "Hi-tech (marketing) is hi-tech burnout, unless you get recharged."

Bully for Sculley. And, lagging managers, mark well this trend. On a personal note, just to show that not all good ideas come from California, let me share with you one of the best business decisions I ever made.

About 20 years ago, I named Morgan Browne President and Chief Operating Officer of Bill Communications, Inc. His chief hobbies were extensive reading and traveling. Thus, I attached one prime condition to the job: Each year, after taking his normal vacation, he was to recharge himself by pursuing personal travel interests for at least three consecutive weeks.

That he did, though he sometimes sneaked back a tad early or pursued an accounts receivable in far-off Spain or

Italy. One payoff was that Bill Communications showed consecutive increased earnings for every year that Browne took a sabbatical. Sure, there have been many other vital contributions that made our company a success, but our trend-setting presidential sabbatical policy was one of the keys.

Top executives are, by nature, workaholics. If you don't force them to take sabbaticals, they'll stay put at the home office—whether they work at their desks or manage by walking around. The surveys show, by the way, that American managers feel guilty when they're out of the office.

I've already pointed to year-after-year of increased earnings as an accomplishment of this sabbatical policy. But even if my company had had a less spectacular record, who's to say that sabbaticals are counterproductive?

Sabbaticals can combat burnout, which is an insidious attack on your company's bottom line. A worn-out manager can lose his desire to go that one step further—to seek that one extra edge of excellence.

Taking one of those extra steps, I encouraged other department leaders, in our decentralized organization, to provide similar sabbaticals for their top people.

Consider the "kick" move as one more element of continuing education. It's the perfect complement to the T-groups, the AMA conferences, the B-school seminars on Executive Education, and specials like Grid training.

Consider also the fact that my top manager had to organize the restructuring of his department to operate in his absence! Look at the benefits of management experience that were reaped by his subordinates filling the void during this absence.

Such is one more example, indirectly, of turning the organizational chart upside down and then throwing it out.

My manager's departure also established restructured roles for him and for those under him. We not only threw out the table of organization, but we threw out the "tops down" job descriptions (JDs) as well. New JDs were instead developed participatively.

In effect, the "kicking" did not stop with the top manager. (Just as in bowling, no matter how hard you try, there's no way you can knock down "only" the Number One pin.)

And while we're on the subject of the domino effect, remember that Unconventional Managers can use other forms of "kicking" to boot.

Take financial managers, for example (at times, the feeling of your line managers may be: "Yes, go ahead and take them—far away," to paraphrase Henny Youngman's "Take my wife.").

Instead of "kicking" a financial manager out of the office, why not kick him into an anticipatory role, working hand-in-hand with line managers?

Kick that financial manager into participating to find money (for raises, business trips, etc.)—instead of letting him be restrictive with the oft-heard negative phrase "No. It's not in the budget."

*—November 1991*

## The First "Ugly American"?

Hans Gunther, a Colgate alum and an old friend of mine, was born with a name that is obviously German. A call from him recently brought back a chuckle. And a reminder when not to be too stuffily precise.

I was born a friendly Midwesterner, then raised/educated/in business in the courtly South. I learned that skills in social conversation are helpful in breaking the ice. But at times I goof. Gunther brought back the memory of one of my international failures, and recoveries.

"John," said Gunther, "I've never asked you before, but isn't 'Hartman' a name of German origin?"

"Jawohl!" I replied, and then I started laughing.

"Hans, you've reminded me of one of my first business-ambassadorial trips to Northern Europe. I'm afraid I took myself much too seriously . . . ."

In the early 1960s I was charged with developing contacts and new members for the Young Presidents' Organization (YPO). These fine folks overseas wanted to be friendly, too, although they didn't know quite what was expected. So their business-leader hosts and hostesses entertained us often at their homes. Our first traveling seminar was to the Scandinavian countries; Sweden first stop. The opening evening, our Swedish host greeted me.

"Ah! 'Hartman!' that's a Swedish origin name, I believe?"

Me—being thick, square, and very naïve—very earnestly replied, "No, sorry. In fact, I think my great-grandfather came from North Germany, not Sweden."

Ugh. My host's welcoming smile froze. End of our social chit-chat.

Next country—Norway. "Oh, yes!" Our Norwegian host noted, "'Hartman' is a Norwegian name?"

"Well, ah, no . . . ," my conventional reply began. But

before I could finish, this time I felt an ankle kick and found myself being tugged away by my wife. I was given The Word (The Unconventional Word).

By the time we reached Denmark and Finland, I'd been well retrained. You name the country, and indeed, if you say so, the "Hartman Family" was also part of a shared past.

Did my unconventional responses skirt the truth?

Absolutely. But today, there are about 2,000 European members of the YPO. I'd like to think my wife's giving me an early kick into a more sociable "hands across the sea" made a little difference . . . and helped broaden the membership.

*—December 1990*

## Why Your Saturday Newspaper Is Different

"Saturday newspapers must be aimed at a small audience of lonely newspaper addicts. They have the smallest circulation (and ad volume) of the week," observes *New York Times* columnist Russell Baker. "Why? Because, for one thing, many potential readers have become too exhausted from Friday night excesses to read anything. For another, because many readers are traveling to the seashore, the mountains, or grandmom's house."

All true. But tell me why I enjoy and look forward to the Saturday *New York Times* even more than all the other six days? There is another reason Baker doesn't understand—one I learned about two decades ago at Harvard Business School.

Today, business research is dominated by polling and focus groups. Further wisdom often comes from research teams of students—subsidized by the inquiring company. These, in turn, often become case history fodder for Harvard B-School projects. I first learned at Harvard about how the *New York Times* worked to become a "national" newspaper, publishing almost simultaneously in Los Angeles, Miami, and New York. One obstacle was the need for three separate editorial staffs—for the Sunday paper; the Monday through Friday editions; and for the leftover Saturday special.

This throwaway Saturday paper thus became the editorial/reportorial proving ground for the tyros of the press. The dissidents, the innovators, and the unconventional provided a Saturday paper that stood out from the rest—with a distinctive verve and a unique appeal.

So, frankly, I don't mind when I miss my Tuesday *Times*. But I dare anyone to try to steal the Saturday paper from my front lawn.

*—June 1995*

# VIEWPOINTS FROM OTHER MAVERICKS

## People & Resources

## Fitting Round Pegs Into Square Holes

In small and small-to-medium companies finding good employees at minimum cost is essential to successful operation. As a division manager of a small-to-medium publishing company, and later general manager of a small company, one trick I learned was the art of fitting round pegs into square holes instead of square pegs into round holes—a discovery that became a vital part of both successful operations.

At the metropolitan daily I managed, I was looking for another business writer, a beginner with some indication of potential. After running the appropriate ad, we were flooded with applicants; none of whom had any demonstrated writing skills or knowledge of the business world.

The deadline for filling the job and getting on to the next step in our rebuilding process was rapidly approaching. I had one application from a young lady recently graduated from one of the country's top journalism schools. There were two fascinating things about her application: (1) Her birthday was the same as mine, and (2) under "Clubs" she had listed "The Book of the Month Club." Was she creative or naïve?

I decided to chance it. She turned out to be, with a little coaxing, a sound hire. In addition to having fine writing skills, she had the necessary people skills to get along in the business world at a time when women were just getting their feet in the door. Eventually she developed a relationship with a top political figure in the town and had her hand firmly on the pulse of the community. Today, she is Assistant Managing Editor of the newspaper.

At the weekly newspaper level, on a paper I founded, growth of a new publication had reached that point beyond which I could handle it all. I needed a good editorial assistant, but had little money to pay one. I opted for hiring a data entry clerk at bottom scale to enter stories and information to speed up my editing process.

During one interview, I learned the job applicant had a Philosophy degree from a small Midwestern college. He had spent the past year touring the country with a professor friend. They had purchased a hot dog wagon and done the carnival circuit. He applied for the job in pony tail, shorts and sandals, sat down at a computer and quickly demonstrated that he was capable of typing over 100 words per minute. I asked why he would consider a $5-an-hour job. His reply: "I'm looking for something new and like this part of the country."

I hired him and found out he had the unusual capacity for instant learning. (I gave him the *Associated Press Style Book* to study and within a week he had it mastered.)

Over the next two years, I raised him to be our managing editor. He performed yeoman's duties with master's skills. He is the heart of that newspaper today with one small shortcoming: He refuses to be concerned, or have anything to do with, the money side of the operation.

I had hoped, when I sold the newspaper, to see him elevated to the new general manager position, but he shot himself in the foot during his first interview with the new owners. Despite my prompting him to the contrary, he ( still wearing his pony tail but dressed by now in long trousers and clean, white sneakers) told them he did not want to be concerned about the money side of the business. The short of it is that they will have a fine managing editor as long as he remains with them; and unless he has a new awakening about the business side of publishing, he may not have a long tenure with his new bosses.

Some round pegs fit into square holes better than others, but my experience has been it is worth taking a look at them and taking the time to work with their idiosyncrasies if you have a hole to fill and find your resources limited.

*—David Whitney*
*Executive Director*
*Pigeon Key Foundation*

## Sure . . . I'll Be Right Down To *Your* Office

I remember once at a Harvard Business School Young Presidents Organization Session, Henry Kotkins reported that he learned a great deal about his employees by reviewing where they cashed their paychecks, by studying the backs of the checks when they were returned from the bank.

John Rollins reported that when he was both Lieutenant Governor of Delaware and operating his various enterprises, including particularly, as I recall, an automobile enterprise, he would make all his political appointments for Thursday afternoon. The rest of the week he would be free to do as he wanted in his business and in politics. And on Thursday afternoon, when people came in and saw an office full of others waiting for him, they would take very little of his time seeing that he was so busy. Whereas, had they come in without an office full of people, they may have taken far more time than he wanted to give them.

The only unconventional, or semi-unconventional practice that I have is to almost always visit people working for and with me in their offices rather than in my own. I have found this makes them more comfortable and bridges a little bit the natural gap between boss and subordinate. If someone in our offices calls and says: "Can I see you about . . . ," I respond: "Sure, I'll be right down."

*—Roger Sonnabend*
*Chairman and CEO*
*Sonesta International*
*Hotels Corporation*

## Seek And Enjoy Risk

When David Finn and I started the business [Ruder & Finn public relations] we decided that we would tithe ourselves 10% of our billable time to use pro bono on behalf of unfinanced causes and institutions about which we felt strongly. We did that for 30 years. It was enormously satisfying and, incidentally, proved to be very sound business. It became a window through which we saw a wider part of the world and met many bright and significant opinion leaders.

In about 1960, I started a separate company (not for profit 501[c] 3) called PIPR, which stands for Public Interest Public Relations. It was seeded by Ford, Kaplan and other foundations to permit this small PR firm to take on some of the highly financed Goliaths in arguing their causes in the public forum. It was enormously successful and in a slightly revised form it continues to exist today.

When one is in the service business and in a situation when we think soliciting a new client is a competitive undertaking, we are often called upon to run "dog and pony shows." I would never do it. I went by myself, and I told them what I thought. They made their own decisions without cosmetics. After we were in business for only 10 years, we became the largest PR firm in the country. So it worked. (Of course, I should add that I left Ruder & Finn in 1980, and it's not the largest firm in the business any more. But it certainly had its Glory Days.)

When we started the company, David and I were very young. It was unthinkable for anybody to call us by anything except our first names. To this day, that's still the rule (I keep my office on their premises) and even the mail boy calls me Bill. I enjoy it, and I think it does something special for the environment.

Our field—public affairs and public relations—is normally characterized by the need to help clients protect the status quo. We long ago decided that this did not fit our personalities and that our purpose was to be change agents. That's a high risk point of view. And so is opening your own business when you are 26 years old and your wife is pregnant. Being an entrepreneur—a good one—means both seeking and enjoying risk. If you don't think that you would absolutely bust if you didn't start you own business, don't do it.

*—Bill Ruder*
*Founder, Ruder & Finn*

## Privacy

We live in a time where the reality of modern business requires a degree of intrusion into the private life of employees. Courts routinely require payroll deductions for child support, even in cases where responsible spouses make timely payments. The hazards of sidestream smoke in the workplace require companies to restrict tobacco use more severely. Companies often are providing employee wellness counseling, psychological assistance, drug screening and accident reporting, which may include more required blood, breath, hearing and eye testing. Companies must require the disclosure of medical conditions and prescription medication that could endanger the worker, himself or others. The age of computers makes it more tempting to micro-manage employee productivity, attendance, work attitude, skills, aptitudes and attendance-adjusted seniority—all in the name of containing corporate costs and promoting employee productivity.

Employee safety often requires TV cameras in the parking lots and fenced controlled points of access from company property. There are more stringent regulations about hard hats, ear protectors, safety glasses with side shields, steel-toed shoes and food in the workplace. Companies that ignore these modern practices do so at their own peril.

Yet, it is the responsibility of the manager to realize that all these factors conspire to make the employee feel more controlled, spied upon, poked, prodded and analyzed. At the margin, the modern factory worker can feel jailed. With apologies to George Orwell, the feeling can be "big brother is watching," and the relationship between company and worker suffers.

There probably isn't a complete cure, but companies must work at staying out of employees' lives when it serves no absolutely necessary purpose. Why have company day care, for example, with the personal intrusions that entails, when you can encourage independent day care not controlled by the company? Is payroll deducting for charitable contributions really necessary, or is it an additional intrusion on ground the company could avoid?

The answers will vary with circumstance, but in the years ahead companies must roll back intrusion whenever they are able if we are to have a balanced adult relationship between management and the rest of the corporate "team." Good luck at finding the balance. Good luck in being a defender of employee privacy whenever that privacy can be safeguarded or enhanced.

*—Jim Dickie II*
*President*
*Crown Equipment*

## Imemyosis: A Fungus Among Us!

The difference between a leader and a boss is the difference between good and bad management. If you are a boss, these words are directed to you. If you have one, you might want to plant a copy of this somewhere in his or her Throne Room.

There is an occupational disease that afflicts all *bosses* and some otherwise good managers, but no true leaders. It is called *Imemyosis* (I-ME-MY-OSIS), a not so rare malady that attacks the central nervous system of good leadership.

Its symptoms are excess use of the words, I, ME and MY in place of WE, US and OUR. (Examples: "I have a break-even point of X dollars a month." "Hey, what are you gonna do for *me* today?" plus a whole litany of puffwords like *my* team, *my* goals, *my* office and *my* people.)

This affliction is also known as the "Narcissus Syndrome" and "Bossitis." It is characterized by a severe swelling of the ego, accompanied by an excessive use of the first person singular in discussing most of the good things that happen within an organization, be it large or small.

It sneaks up on otherwise normal and caring supervisors who are, in most cases, unaware of the unpleasant image it projects to their customers and colleagues.

Let's face it: excessive use of the first person singular is not only unattractive and offensive to others, it is built on an inaccurate presumption.

By definition, a leader/manager is one who get things done through the efforts of others and, as a Chinese philosopher once wrote, "When the true leader's work is done, the people say 'We did it ourselves!'"

There is a high probability that many "imemyotic" managers rely on the I and Me and My as a reminder to all that they *are* the boss, and it is just as probable that this often disguises an unsure self-image.

It should never be necessary to remind your followers that you are their leader. They should already recognize you as such, and if they do not, your claim to be one is a pointless (and probably counter-productive) effort.

As to others outside the team, it serves no purpose to flash your stars and bars. If they don't think you're important, telling them you are won't make much difference.

I like this story, which may or may not be true, about Joe Louis: long after his days of glory as a boxing champion, he and a small entourage entered a restaurant in New York and were asked to wait behind the velvet cord.

One of Joe's companions was angered at what he considered a slight to the former champ, so he said, "Joe, tell them who you is!" And Louis is said to have replied, "When you gotta tell 'em who you *is*, you *ain't*."

It is the very essence of good leadership to give away all credit to positive achievement, to identify only *team* goals and always to refer to them as such.

Those who are after personal glory and adulation in management positions have selected the wrong vocation.

*—Joseph Klock*
*Realtor, columnist*

## Giving The Extra Ounce

Even as a boy, I was an observer of people. I watched them in every phase of their lives, studying them, and questioning why they did certain things—and what impact those things had on their happiness and level of success. I was strongly impressed by the discovery that the moderately successful person did nearly as much work as the outstandingly successful one. The difference in effort was quite small—only an "extra ounce." But the results, in terms of accomplishment and the quality of the achievement, were often dramatic.

I came to call this principle the "doctrine of the extra ounce." And I quickly noticed that the doctrine was confined not to just one field of endeavor but could be applied in all fields. In fact, it seemed be a kind of universal principle that could lead to success in life.

For example, when it came to high school football games, I discovered that the boys who tried a little harder and practiced a little more became the stars. They contributed the key plays that won games. They tended to be the ones who gained the support of the fans and were complimented by the coaches. And all because they did just a *little* bit more than their teammates.

I also observed the doctrine of the extra ounce at work in my high school classrooms. Those who did their lessons reasonably well received good grades. But those who did their lessons a little bit better than anyone else—who exerted the extra ounce—received top grades and all the honors.

The same principle applied at Yale. I made sure that I had my lessons not just 95 percent right but 99 percent right. The result? I got into Phi Beta Kappa in my junior year and was elected president of the Yale chapter—an accomplishment that had a significant part in my being selected for a Rhodes scholarship.

Out in the business world, I refined my doctrine further.

I came to realize that giving that single extra ounce results in better quality. Those who try harder are capable of a higher level of performance. And the person who gives seventeen ounces to the pint rather than sixteen will achieve rewards all out of proportion to that one ounce.

The doctrine of the extra ounce is particularly noticeable in professional sports. Some will give their very heart and soul on the baseball diamond, and they are highly rewarded for their supreme efforts. Pete Rose is a perfect example. He may not have been the most talented player on the field, but his genius lay in giving top effort.

In order to promote an attitude of the extra ounce, it has been my practice for more than 30 years to pay employees about 20 percent above the current trade salary levels. That's not the result of kindheartedness. Rather, it's the belief that if you pay 20 percent more than normal, you will gradually accumulate a superior team; for 20 percent more money, you will field a team that is 50 percent more effective. "You get what you pay for," I tell those who doubt me. "The old adage is true."

However, there are times when you will make an error in judgment; you will find that some people on your team do not pull their own weight. In such cases I don't recommend that you adopt the charitable view and swallow your mistake, nor do I believe in taking a cutthroat, unloving attitude. Once having admitted the mistake, you should try to find an area in which those employees are proficient and shift them into it. If you can't find such a spot in your own organization, find it in someone else's. Then you can go to the employees and explain that while what they are doing presently is neither to their own or the company's advantage, you have found a slot for them where they have a chance to become important and successful people.

*—Sir John Templeton*
*Founder*
*Templeton Growth Fund*

## Eccentric Moves

In 1981, I followed Jock Elliott as the next Chairman/CEO of Ogilvy & Mather International, the fourth largest agency in the world with billings then of just under $2 billion. (Jock had followed the legendary David Ogilvy, already living in France.)

As David before him, Jock, now the retired chairman, asked to move to a small office down the hall. At a short meeting (standing up) my response to Jock was: "Stay here. If you move four or five other people will want to move, at a cost of over $200,000. We'll all be happy where we are for quite awhile."

It worked. Jock didn't object. No moves. And, somehow the agency tripled its billings in the next seven years—and then moved all offices to a new building.

*—William Phillips*
*Former Chairman & CEO*
*Ogilvy & Mather*

# PART TWO

# Management

## Accentuate The Positive; De-emphasize The Negative

If you're older than age 55, surely you'll remember the music that accompanied our homework studies—and that drove our exasperated parents nuts.

Remember "Accent-u-ate the Positive . . . E-lim-innate the Negative"? Our parents will swear they endured our blaring radios with it on the Hit Parade for ten years. Well, for sure, it was top ten for ten months.

This all came back to me recently. In kind of a "junior morality play" I was trying to share with some of my children and their spouses some of my own frustrations in previously learning—the hard way—that the world is usually gray . . . not pure black or white. Remember the next line of "Accent?" It is: "Don't mess with Mr. In-Between."

To me, that's true if you insist all compromise in life is weak, to be rejected. But, I suggest a compromise is still a "yes, but;" and there is always more merit in accenting the positive.

I tried to urge my progeny to go back to the message of the opening "Accent the Positive" line. To me, negatives can't enhance family values, lifestyles, Gross National Product—really anything. We find most things in life are really black as well as white, Yin as well as Yang. Further, all of us, without exception, have been put together with both these positive and negative persona.

I wish I could say all this was apparent to me 45 years ago when I was starting out on my own. It was at an advertising agency in northern Florida. An elderly family friend had retired after an extraordinarily successful career as a media/advertising top executive. Call him "Clair." Clair inevitably became a personal and business hero and role model.

Then, suddenly, my bright-eyed, bushy-tailed naïve optimism was devastated. Some human frailties of Clair's began to emerge. The rationale was that it was his aging and change of life problems. Regardless, all of a sudden I had Clair aspects that I didn't like, couldn't understand, didn't want to relate to. Unwillingly, I found myself denigrating everything he said. I started looking for the holes in Clair, ignoring the cheese. We became estranged. My disillusionment with Clair continued for some months. Then, something triggered a re-examination, a questioning of myself:

"John, 15 percent of Clair's lifestyles and practices are an enigma to you. Appalling, or you don't approve. Right?"

"Right."

"But the other 85 percent of Clair, you reaffirm, is warm, well-intentioned, constructive, good-hearted, unselfish, giving?"

"Yes, I agree."

"John, which then do you want to concentrate upon? Wallow with the 15 percent negative? Or the 85 percent positive?"

I took another look, adjusted, grew up a little more. It was to become a major lesson for me in tolerance and values. We again became friends, sharing and learning from each other until his death.

**Life Too Short For Negatives**

Of course, sermons by elders like this inevitably are suffered by our youngsters. The eyes roll skywards, and with some justification. It is their life and value styles to be determined. Still, all elders humanely hope some of their experiences, such as "Clair," can somehow be cranked into the kids' decision making.

For me, the "take-Clair-on-the-batting-average-perception" was a major philosophical breakthrough—one I've carried with me and returned to for the rest of my life. Rarely have I been disappointed by such faith. The positive response far outweighs the rare negatives.

So? So the theme of this small "morality play" is to encourage our I-can-do-it-myself youngers to continue to tolerate their well-intentioned elders' attempts to pass on pearls of wisdom.

Right, wrong or even "Mr. In-Between" remember it's the batting average that counts most. And just one hit out of three at bats often wins a major league batting title.

*—August 1994*

## Management Styles . . . I Or We?

We've been getting feedback from Ocean Reef golf and tennis foursomes on a previous column noting a shift in politics and business from authoritarian to participative management.

Not all agree that it's a desirable trend, of course. And I, too, agree that there are times when you've got to cut through the committees and say: "Gentlemen, here's our new letterhead. Next subject."

One problem for us in abandoning Authoritarian Management is that it is how much of America got built. Henry Ford ("You can have any color you want, just so it's black") production assembly lines, Teddy-FDR-Daddy Warbucks, the Catholic and Protestant churches. Winnie, Ike and Marshall won World War II with authoritarian-military-style management. Though, arguably, the precursor of Participative Management was even then emerging as uniquely American . . . unthinkable then by the rigid Teutonic Germans. I refer to our secret weapon: The Midnight Requisition, which bypassed official channels to get the mission accomplished

Many of today's executives still swear by the Table of Organization, likened to a Christmas tree with Authority, Wisdom and Decisions trickling down from the top to the layered, less wise "workers" below. "I'm the boss . . . my title says I'm the planner . . . I'll make the decisions . . . just do as I say." Indeed, for many financial/accounting functions dealing primarily in tangibles (less so with people), Participative Management may just not be practical.

Anyway, in the 1950s Harvard Business School's original management guru, the late Professor Douglas McGregor, labeled Authoritative Management as Theory X.

We have been long exposed to various forms of Participative Management. Japan used it and went from producing distress-sale merchandise to top quality. No, you skeptics, it's not committees. But, it is sometimes collegial, often bottoms-up ideas, always top-down pushing of decisions, risking the right to be wrong, on the nine-point Grid scale a 9:9 on equal concern for people and productivity. McGregor called these characteristics "Theory Y."

One of my primary mentors in all this theorem back in the very early 1960s was Harvard B-School's professor Abe Zaleznik, inheritor of McGregor's mantle. Abe taught a five-day refresher course at Harvard on new and old management disciplines for the Young Presidents' Organization (YPO)

In those days, some of us found this "nice but firm . . . what do you think?" Theory Y management style more than awkward to embrace. There was a practical reason. Depression-background families all, many of us doubted we would have had our businesses survive healthy enough for YPO membership eligibility, if we hadn't been pretty authoritarian.

My friend Dillard Munford, a Southerner's Southerner from Atlanta, was one of these. Dillard had bootstrapped his company into a NYSE retail octopus. Fortunately, he knew little about our business, unlike our other outside director, Warren "Good Cop" McClure. So, I prevailed upon Dillard to be our always-questioning, hard-nosed "Bad Cop" director. It was an effective balance, with Dillard always smiling and joking on the outside but turning the screws with tough questions to our managers and inside directors.

Back to our Harvard B-School class. On the last day Dillard raised his hand for attention: "Perfessor! I think I've got this Theory Y and Theory X stuff figured out right well."

"Good, Dillard," replied Zaleznik. "Would you sum up for all of our class?"

Dillard grinned. "Well, Theory X is when I see a mess in the plant and I tell the SOB responsible: "Get off your A and get that cleaned up. Right?"

"Right on, Dillard. And Theory Y?"

"Now that's when we have the same mess, same guy. But this time I put my arm around his shoulders in a caring manner, point to the mess and say, 'Clean it up . . . suh!'"

The maybe moral? Sometimes it takes a Theory X hard nose to "jump-start" a Theory Y participative culture.

*—July 1990*

## When To Switch Back From 'We' To 'I'

Total quality management, re-engineering, downsizing, target-marketing, just-in-time-inventories, quality circles, marketing myopia, plan-your-work then work-your-plan and others . . . are all current and past business buzzwords. Some have had a longer shelf-life than others.

Probably the most enduring has been the concept of "Participative Management." Its origins are usually traced back to the management experiments in 1928 of General Electric in its Hawthorne plant. It was found that workers who could participate in making their own work rules were more productive. General Motors' Alfred P. Sloan decentralized (by definition, more participative) production, sales and marketing and revolutionized the automotive industry. Douglas McGregor gave the movement great impetus with his Theory X (hard-nosed authoritarian) and Theory Y (participative) styles of management. Harvard Business School's Abe Zaleznik picked up the torch after McGregor died. Bob Blake gave renewed life to McGregor's theorems putting X and Y on a nine-point grid.

I was first inoculated with the "participative management virus" in 1962. It was at a Young Presidents Organization sponsored then pioneer T-Group (T stands for Training) for 13 fellow business executives. For all of us the new alternative of participative rather than authoritarian management became the dawn of the application of the Behavioral Sciences to business. As a leading advocate and practitioner of decentralization, my company's applications of "Bottoms-Up Tables of Organization" are still used in Harvard Business School Case Studies. I lectured on the subject at Harvard, Duke University, The American Management Association's President Association. Yes, it even overlapped into my home and social life. My ever-indulgent family and tennis and golf colleagues groaned and rolled with my newly found enthusiasms for participative management. But it generally worked.

**Limits Of Democracy**

All this was and is good and true, probably the way of the future as well. But, a caution. Even McGregor, Sloan, Zaleznik and Blake advise some flexibility and limitations. Let me illustrate with an anecdote about the late Carroll Busby, former CEO of Chilton—the major business-to-business publishing company. Until Busby's era, with some exceptions, most of Chilton's entries were perceived as somewhat stodgy second or third-rate business magazines. His task was to revive them and meet the post World War II challenges. In many ways Busby accomplished this with participative management techniques, pushing decision-making down the line.

At the time, being junior to him by 30 years, at every opportunity I used to pick Busby's brains, particularly about participative management. But one time, when we were on a train to a Washington, D.C. conference together, Busby must have felt I was going a little overboard. He interrupted my enthusiasm to caution: "John. I share your zeal for participative management. It's more than a passing business buzzword. But, democracy in management does have its limitations. It's not a panacea."

"How so?" I asked.

"Let me give you an example. Not long ago I decided Chilton needed a new corporate letterhead. So I made all the right participatory moves: preliminary and advisory committees, involvement of diverse managers . . . outside consultants, whatever."

Busby, also a talented showman from his Princeton Glee Club days, and one of the last masters of the five-string banjo, reached for that instrument from the train seat alongside him. He strummed it once.

"But days went by, time was consumed with ten different

designs, without being able to arrive at a consensus decision on the new letterhead," Busby continued. "So I assembled our participating managers, told them we had to resolve this and move on, reached for a design I liked, and held it up, saying:

"'Gentlemen, your new letterhead.'"

Busby strummed his banjo three times.

*—July 1994*

## Reconciling Participative And Authoritarian Management

When I got hooked in the early sixties, "Participative Management" was brand new. Now it's a popular business buzzword. Today, hardly anyone makes an advertising or marketing muscle move without the guidance of a Focus Group, by definition "participative."

Bitten by the participative bug, it became for me the wave of the future for business management. It included the Quality Circle concept before that practice even had a label. It seemed clear it would become the most important managerial development since General Motors' Alfred P. Sloan in the 1920s revolutionized corporate tables of organization by introducing effective decentralization . . . also, by definition, more participative. Interestingly, a recent *Advertising Age* article (Sept. 20, 1993) headlines: "Time, Inc. Is Shaking Up Its Corporate Structure—Again," and notes: "the reorganization includes decentralizing many corporate functions . . . ."

My participative convictions were reinforced in the 1960s by attendance in National Training Laboratory's T-Groups and Scientific Methods Grid Schools. Harvard Business School reportedly still uses case histories describing my experiences with implementing participative management throughout my companies. I still believe it is the way to go.

### Malingerers Don't Get It

But. There's always a big "but," isn't there! Participative is still too often wrongheadedly disparaged as diminishing the role of a strong, individual authority figure, make-a-difference leader. However, I say the malingerers just don't get it. Rather, my observation is that only strong leadership can induce the conditions and environment for the more effective participative management to work.

Just what is the "Big Daddy" type of thinking? In government it is that central leadership knows best. Symbolized by communism, it is failing everywhere. The remaining European Socialist countries' governments are in minority disarray in the polls, North Korea and Cuba cling on, for the moment. Even Poland's newly elected ex-communist leaders and the opposition in Russia promise democratic decentralized reforms, only at a slower pace of introduction. And even the current "constitutional despotism" of Peru and Venezuela is still subject to a people's referendum.

In business, the former titans keep tumbling as they desperately try new downsizing, decentralizing handles for mere survival. Our "bigger is better" authoritarian role models of only a decade ago continue to lose market share: GM, IBM, Sears, American Airlines.

Remember those conventional wisdoms, now blown, those bigger buzzwords of the 1980s? "Let's merge" . . . "throw money at it" . . . "acquire it for our own conglomeration" . . . "get bigger by buying them with their own debt (LBOs)" . . . "force the market into our own one-stop, one-shop accumulations of services" (à la Saatchi & Saatchi advertising/consulting).

What do all the above buzzwords have in common? They have largely proved to be hogwash, demonstrable intellectual rubbish. Blinkered by globalization, those seeking business sought solutions based on increasing volume and mass marketing. Some, inevitably including the federal governments, are still slow to catch on to failures of mass, top-down thinking, Yes, the markets worldwide are getting larger, but they are simultaneously getting more selective in their receptivity to ideas—in business or governance.

Recently the normally more perceptive *Newsweek* magazine editorialized to the effect: "Only the government can bring the blacks (as markets) into the mainstream . . . ." Yet, weirdly the same issue rebutted this premise in their own poll of blacks who answered *Newsweek's* question: "Which can do the most to improve the situation for black families today?" Eighty-one percent gave a "participative" answer, with 41 percent saying "black families themselves," 26 percent saying "churches," 14 percent naming "community organizations." Only 14 percent said authoritarian "Big Daddy top-down government."

### Marketing-To-Be-Bigger Plans Backfire

Until the 1980s, Sears was one of the Top 10 business role models. Business chains wisely focused on locations adjacent to Sears outlets. The faithfully repeated and followed litany of Sears' customers was the then motto: "Sears For Service."

Then, the Sears marketeers of the moment, perhaps bored with success and seeking to build new monuments to themselves, in an authoritarian mode decided consumers could be made to be interested in One-Stop Shopping. While customers were picking up a refrigerator, tire or hammer they could also waltz down the aisles to buy Allstate insurance or stocks and investments through Dean Witter. The idea seemed a knee-slapper at the time for the Sears financial efficiency planners but proved to be a flop in the marketplace.

The production/mass-driven market thinking—instead of customer service sales orientation—also accounted for many of the failures in the 1980s of the LBOs and non-related acquisitions by conglomerates.

But things are changing. "Business Giants Hope To Score Big By Looking Small" is the headline of a *Wall Street Journal* report, The article's lead is "Big business' courtship with the small(er) business customer is turning ardent" and concludes with " . . . once proud IBM, which is struggling through a massive reorganization . . . says: 'We (now) take customer satisfaction (again, participative by definition) very seriously and have been working hard to improve our responsiveness.'"

"Big Daddy" may think he knows best in selling people on government and marketing products and services. But, clearly in the 1990s the customers who pay the bills are becoming more selective in their responses. Target marketing is replacing mass.

### Flip Side Of Participation

A recent article celebrates the 80th birthday of California's most famous marketer of wines, vintner Robert Mondavi. Julia Child, author and chef, is quoted: "Thanks to him, marketing of California wines got started. Before him in the 1960s, they were a laughing stock. In a short time Mondavi accomplished what it took the Europeans hundreds of years to do."

Our business, marketing, advertising and cultural history is full of individual leaders who clearly made a difference: Eisenhower, GM's Sloan, Apple's Steve Jobs, and (in his pioneer days) Poland's Lech Walesa, Lenin, Russia's Gorbachev and maybe Yeltsin, David Ogilvy, Churchill, FDR, Reagan, IBM's Tom Watsons-Sr. and Jr.

But, study all the successes. You won't find among them a single one with an authoritative do-it-only-my-way-as-I-say style. Instead they were the leaders in setting the tone and climate for a more effective involved, creative, committed participative management. Even Christ has his disciples.

—*December 1993*

## Golden Ground Rules For Unconventional Thinkers

If you've been around long enough, chances are you were drilled during the school week on the basics: readin', writin' and 'rithmetic. On Sunday, the curriculum was the Golden Rule: "Do unto others as you would have them do unto you."

Of course, a very few of your contemporaries may have grown into cynics, and changed it to "Do unto others before they do you in."

But, for the overwhelming majority of our business and personal associations, we're happy to report the Golden Rule prevails. Most of the time.

We were pleasantly reminded of this the other day when we read an editorial by a magazine publisher named Charles L. Wrye. Noting he has served successively with three fine publishing companies (Time, Inc., Scholastic Publications, and Bill Communications, Inc.), Wrye called attention to "an unusual document" that helped guide his most recent company: "Golden Ground Rules For Unconventional Managers."

"These simple rules, developed 27 years ago—but still operative—are seldom practiced in other companies," said Wrye. "But here they have helped breed success and fierce employee loyalties. We try to follow these Ground Rules in all our business dealings—internally among ourselves, and externally with our readers, advisers, and suppliers."

Many thanks to Chuck Wrye. My personal goal is to help preserve those rules in print. They are:

1. Always give your fellow employee credit for good intentions, allowing for poor communications and sometimes poor execution.

2. Disagree behind closed doors and try to give, and to get, an honest understanding of viewpoints.
3. It is only fair to company associates that the management team present a united front. If a decision must be reconsidered, get behind closed doors again before indicating that it will be changed.
4. Remember that people will complain, especially about trivia, and it is not necessarily unhealthy. Many statements disguised as complaints are really questions asking for guidance or reassurance.
5. Talk to others, and write memos, without seeming aggressive. Listen to others, and read their memos, without seeming defensive.
6. Don't hesitate to overcommunicate when the information is good or positive. Send few, if any, carbons when it is bad or negative.
7. Truth, honesty, objectivity, personal and corporate excellence, and mutual respect are the framework of our company's management. Within this framework all decisions should be made and executed, all controversies resolved.
8. The true professional observes these rules even when tired, pressed, overworked, or facing deadlines. In order to manage others, one must first manage oneself.

*—May 1991*

## Gettin' 'Em To The Meetin' Hall On Time

An unconventional manager has to be a jack-of-all trades, involved in many activities. So, this one's for you whenever you're assigned the responsibility of being the planner for one of your company's out-of-town conferences.

All that hard work has narrowed down to a precious few days that are at last upon you. For you, it's the opening of the conference/convention you've been involved in planning for months. You've arranged for faculty and resources, their Just In Case backups, hotel and air negotiations, seminar rooms, directional-informational signs, sound systems, bands and entertainment, afternoon sports and pool side roundtables—whew! All systems are at last "GO!"

But, hold on. There's one possible hitch. The vast majority of your attendees these days take the business sessions seriously. Usually, they'll handle themselves by being there on time. But, every year there's an anxious countdown concern for a significant minority. Will the "night" people arise and make the morning business sessions that are scheduled in advance of the coffee break? Will your speaker be embarrassed by not enough bodies to fill the first 14 rows?

You can depend upon your Welcoming Committee to have done a good indoctrination job at the reception-dinner on Opening Sunday. But sometimes they do too good. Long traveled attendees relax a little too much. The partying and the idea exchanging that goes on much later in the night than usual can exhaust them. The penalty the next morning is Irving Berlin's famous song: "Oh, How I Hate To Get Up In The Morning . . . ."

The challenge now is to get the morning meetings started on time—with the maximum possible number of meeting attendees at least pretending to give their alert attention. For over 40 years I, too, have been one of the meeting planners involved in this key task. I've observed and swiped wake-

'em-up ideas from such diverse groups as the Magazine Publishers Association, American Business Press, American Association of Advertising Agencies, Young Presidents' Organization (and its alumni, the World Business Council and Chief Executives Organization), The Conference Board, American Management Association, and American Newspaper Publishers Association.

That's a mouthful. But, most happily, most of my conferences were at posh watering holes, and none was very hard to take ("somebody's got to do it!" is what we always told our junior personnel). The hardship areas we visited included such as: The Homestead, Dolder Grand, Arizona Biltmore, Williamsburg Inn, Breakers, Boca Raton, Ocean Reef (plus many more an oasis in places like Scottsdale, Palm Springs, Orlando, San Francisco, Bermuda, Nassau, the Caribbean, and Mexico).

**The Best Waker-Upper Ever**

Being retired, I hadn't thought about conference planning until recently. But it all came back when I ran into Art Linkletter during a recent visit to the remarkable Bohemian Grove encampment, two-and-one-half hours north of San Francisco. Those of you who have been to the Grove know well perhaps its greatest reward is the opportunity to renew old friendships from around the country, and make new ones.

Thanks to my host, Tom Bailard, I was doing just that, visiting on a pathway with several old buddies, when one said: "Hey, there goes Linkletter!"

I knew Jack Linkletter as a fellow YPO member and thought it was he, so I called out: "Hi, Linkletter, come join us!" When he stopped and turned, I belatedly realized it was instead Jack's dad, Art, whom I had never met. But everybody is real friendly at Grove outings. Art joined our group and graciously participated in sharing experiences. One story he'd never heard was about his son, Jack.

"Did Jack ever tell you how he got YPOers and spouses

out of bed when he was running his YPO University in Hawaii?" I asked Art.

"No," said Art. "You mean the year he was International President? Tell me, please."

"Best job I ever saw," I replied. "His formula was: Meeting Morning One: Drum and bugle corps and bagpipes marching through the hotel halls at 7:00 A.M. Meeting Morning Two: Helicopter circling 20 feet from our rooms with loud bullhorn. Meeting Morning Three: A loud knock on our doors. Greeting us with a hula band with a lovely Hawaiian dancing lady clad only in a grass skirt. The conventional flower lei was absent. Meeting Mornings Four and Five: 'Okay, Jack, okay. We've got The Word. We're on our own now — and ON TIME.'"

Now there's an unconventional challenge that meeting planners would be hard pressed to top.

*—August 1991*

## Got A Problem?

"How does he react to problem solving?" was one of the questions asked me in a referral about someone who has worked closely with me for several years.

"Well, he travels a lot. So, if you want someone on a yo-yo string, always available, he's not for you," I replied in part. Then I went on about my friend's demonstrated strengths.

But, it got me to thinking about problem solving . . .and the very different ways I've seen folks approach it. Particularly in business, but they apply really across the board, domestically and socially as well. My own problem-solving style preference has been the "What Do You Think?" school. It buys time, involves others in a meaningful way, you might learn something, still you don't have to follow their response. What's to lose?

Yet that isn't the only way to resolve problems, by any means. Following are ten more ways to approach a decision:

• **Big Daddy knows best.** "I am THE manager. The Organization Chart says I'm at the top . . . the boss. I'm paid to manage, not listen. So do as I say." (Let's hope this is going the way of the dodo-bird.)

• **The Boiling Pot Method.** The assumption here is that there are always too many decisions to be made, so just dump them all in a boiling pot. Only those that are most urgent will boil to the surface, to be grabbed and hopefully acted upon. This has some merit in that many boil themselves away even if not acted upon. But it also invites some bloody noses . . .and events running you, rather than otherwise.

• **The Tickler File.** A variation of the "Boiling Pot" that postpones action, but lets you sleep in a more orderly manner. This is also known as a "Ruthless Tickler File," able to stir someone else to action without doing any more at the time yourself.

• **"The ball's in your court."** A good objective. The idea is to avoid final decision, but insure that you have done everything and intimidate others to be responsible for the next action.

• **Benign Neglect**. Much more difficult in days of instant communications, the fax and E-Mail. Lawyers, for instance, used to be able to count on long weekend absences without need to respond to clients from Thursday on, blaming it on slow mail deliveries; no more with the intrepid fax that works even weekends.

• **Neglect Neglect.** Problem is you can only be "out to lunch" so many times before everybody gives up on you. But it will work for some for awhile.

• **"Problem? Whassa problem?"** When you try this just hope you have good support colleagues.

• **The Dart Board.** Don't knock it. Year after year both *Forbes* magazine and the *Wall Street Journal* pit dart board stock picks against the pros. More often than not, the dart board wins.

• **Pro-active Anticipation,** Better than most styles. But make sure you run the system, not the system run you.

• **Loose As A Goose.** Switch styles as needed, depending upon given situations. No rigidity. Be "predictably unpredictable". . . Theory X or the grid's 9:1 (authoritarian) when "the train is leaving the station". . . or Theory Y or grid 9:9 (participative) if there's time.

Whenever possible, I like the latter, combined with "What Do You Think?"

*—September 1994*

## Myths The Successful Manager Avoids

Managers who are top achievers are sometimes mislabeled as "just lucky." Well, "luck" often plays a role in the success of a product or service, but almost never until the marketing is well along.

Luck is often just the better handling of the wholly unanticipated, the unresearched. And it's here—this kind of luck—where the playing field is level for all, be they the established big and mighty companies . . . or the always undercapitalized tyros.

In fact, often the newcomers have some advantage in this area. They are more flexible, can move in (or out) faster. They don't have as much inventory, plant or union-practice baggage.

If you feel safety in following the pack, staying the course, naturally you survive. But to do more—if you are willing to be a maverick, unconventional manager—you have unbounded opportunities.

No, this does not mean being "anti-establishment." It does require a willingness to look at things just a little differently than the conventional wisdoms. Making a difference is usually not on a one-out-of-five home run basis, but on making a lot of singles.

Thus we have our first business myth:

### 1. The Mythical Advantage Of Superpower Business' Planning And Research.

Often at least half of a business success results from the way totally unplanned events are acted upon. It's true in all industries. But let me illustrate with an example from my own world of media:

In the early 1950s, Time, Inc., founder Henry R. Luce's high-riding publishing company needed a new property to help challenge and retain its talented troops. With the advantage of state-of-the-art research and planning, Mr.

Luce's concept this time was an elite sports-participant magazine. Dogmatic about one-name titles, Time spent a lot of money pre-marketing the title "Sports." After a lawsuit by McFadden, already owner of a magazine titled *Sport*, Time, Inc., reluctantly settled for its first two-name title: *Sports Illustrated*. Little did Time imagine that with TV still to emerge, this defeat and the *Illustrated* handle forced upon them would help be their savior many years later.

The founding participant-format couldn't entice enough readers and advertisers. In its first 13 years, *SI* lost $29 million. It was rescued only by the wholly unplanned success of professional football on network TV and the concomitant rise of reader interest in bookmaking. *SI* refashioned itself into a commercially successful "Joe Six-Pack" spectator-only oriented magazine, with special emphasis on the swimsuit issue. (Time, Inc., old-timers are still glad Mr. Luce passed on before seeing this.)

**2. The Myth Of "The Professional Manager Who Could Manage Anything."**

Harold Geneen, post World War II CEO of the temporarily successful conglomerate ITT, which was made up of many disparate parts, was as much responsible as anyone for this canard. In fairness, Mr. Geneen really believed that "A Manager Is A Manager Is A Manager" and could hop from one unrelated business to another with ease.

As companies Mr. Geneen solicited for acquisition learned, he had little time, interest or patience for anything but strictly the financial aspects and controls, People, product, customers and suppliers were, to him, simply commodities to be moved around by the controller. I suggest Mr. Geneen had it a bit wrong.

By producing the "manager who can manage anything—no matter how unrelated," it encouraged that concept's "nephew" in the Excessive Eighties—hostile takeovers and non-strategic acquisitions. Only a handful survive today . . .

and those are massively downsizing.

If Mr. Geneen and the conglomerate kings had done their homework, they would have learned about the studies of Abe Zaleznik and the late Douglas McGregor, both of Harvard Business School, and both pioneers in the behavioral "science" of management. Even with the best training, optimally only 8% of managers have the personality to transfer successfully leadership skills from one industry to another unrelated one. And if they are over the age of 35 when they try, forget it.

Summing up: You can and should train your managers to "Manage Professionally," but that is not at all the same as trying to find and rely upon the rare, true "Professional Manager."

### 3. Management By Objectives (MBO) Is The Answer To Everything Myth.

Peter Drucker's dictum got off to a good start. But, like most, it got twisted, abused. The question disintegrated to "whose objective?"

If it turns out to be solely, or primarily, Management's Objective—without real regard for others (employees, stockholders, community, customers, suppliers)—it proves fallow, or works, at best, with limited success. Embracing others' objectives, as well, is a different story. It is primarily the more recent advance and harnessing of Participative Management concepts that subsequently has validated MBO.

### 4. Planning Is A Straight Line Progression Myth.

The cliché used to be: "We're at Point A and want to get to Point Z. Let's just pick up and go." Or, "continuing this trend line means we will . . . ."

Uh-uh. Doesn't work that way. Remember Business Myth One (above)? At least half of the marketing process will be successfully adjusted to the wholly unanticipated, the unplanned. Thus, in reality the progression line is more of a wobble from Point A, yes, in the general direction to Point Z.

But realistically plan in the interim to go to intermediary points via way-stop stations. At, say, Point D, your next real step is a choice among E-l, E-2, E-3, E-4.

**5. The Management By Exception (MBE) Is Competitive Enough Today Myth.**

This was a popular fad in the 1960s. It sounded good and was written up in B-school case studies The idea is to multiply your managerial self by randomly dipping into operations for unexpected inspections. By lengthening the manager's shadow with surprise shop visits or irregular periodic paperwork micromanaging, the idea is that you can multiply your talents . . . and maybe get an occasional long weekend.

The Japanese changed all that. There is just no way to have "Just-In-Time" inventories, quality circles, involve yourself in Participatory Management and work it by "exception."

**6. The Myth Of Greener Pastures: Better To Acquire Than Build Your Own.**

This is often the philosophy of the short-term oriented executive. Do something (anything) is their preferred route. Some also suggest it is one of the reasons the *Fortune/Forbes* 500 have lost so much market share for the past 20 years. (The New York Stock Exchange lost about 20% of its listed companies to acquisitions during this period.)

Conversely, the more long-term focus of mid-sized businesses has resulted during the same period in the greater relative domestic and export sales growth and Share-of-the-Market. Their slower growth has been more internal (natural), but with greater staying power. Then, too, by "growing your own" you know and can better adapt to your own demons, Acquisitions mean you get all the unknown devils.

**7. The Growth-For-Growth's-Sake vs. Controlled Growth Myth.**

See above.

**8. The "Global Marketing" Myth.**

At least so far, virtually no marketeer has bought the concept (promoted by Saatchi & Saatchi advertising agency) of "One-Stop One-Shop universal product sales and marketing." Our longtime marketing guru friend Ted Levitt has been right on so many things, we prefer to believe Saatchi's crediting the concept to him has resulted in the misrepresentation and the inability to execute. Or just maybe the famous Harvard professor's prescription was prematurely idealistic.

In fact, the fall of the Berlin Wall and the opening up of Europe has intensified—rather than solidified—separatist provincial/nationalistic needs in marketing. Yes, there will be more common and simplified codification of European inventory, transportation customs and product labeling. But don't try selling a recalcitrant Frenchman something in Italian, Swedish, or even English. Not yet.

**9. Not A Myth: Successful Unconventional Managers & Entrepreneurs Will Take Their Ideas As Far As They Can Themselves.**

Sure, it's a given: almost all new enterprises are undercapitalized, outgunned by the biggies. Many fail because too soon they go after supplementary financing from banks, friends, sharks or insurance companies.

It's true: "Never let the green eyeshades into the corner offices." They can be supportive as friends, yes. But not control. Unproductive, uncreative pressures can stifle; stay independent as much and as long as possible.

We opened this article with experiences of Time, Inc.'s founder, Henry Luce. We close with another: Don't pay too much attention to the "experts." Be your own expert. Trust yourself.

*—November 1991*

# VIEWPOINTS FROM OTHER MAVERICKS

## Management

## It's All In The Execution

It's not the idea that's critical; it's the execution. A lousy idea, well executed, murdered six million people. A good idea, badly executed, will not pull the skin off a rice pudding.

*—Brian Wolfson*
*CEO*
*Anglo-Nordic Holdings*

## Agendas, Chapter 11 & Procrastination

When preparing for a business meeting, be sure there is an agenda. A meeting without an agenda is a social event.

Most of the major Ivy League business schools are now teaching "Chapter 11-101." The first thing they advise, if you are going to go into Chapter 11 is to be sure and do it two days before Christmas. You'll find everybody much more receptive, or, they won't even notice it so you can raise the money to get out of it, and your lawyers will have to charge you less.

Finally, if there is something that you yearn to do, do it now. Don't procrastinate another day. Another day may never come.

*—Herman Shepherd*
*Chairman*
*Albert B. Sabin Vaccine*
*Foundation, Inc.*

## The Contrarian Approach

Conventional wisdom says that most, if not all, significant management decisions should be made top down. It also says that global competition is seriously hurting profits, which companies have only limited power to change.

These two points at first blush may seem unconnected, but in fact they go hand-in-hand to damage and limit a company's performance.

Most company decisions may be taken top down, but they should be taken wherever possible where the wisdom and experience reside. Unfortunately the culture, the method of goal setting and the internal reward system at most companies make sure it doesn't happen that way.

### The Objective

In considering these two issues we decided that at Simmonds Precision the enemy was ourselves and certainly not the competition. We agreed to manage unconventionally. We would tap that hidden reservoir of wisdom and experience and change the way we made our decisions. We acknowledged that there was a mine of untapped profits within our company, that we were the impediment and we would learn how to significantly increase the yield.

### Education

With audio-visual aids, I talked to all 3,000 employees directly and explained to them that America was losing the productivity race and becoming increasingly non-competitive. Thirty years of postwar industrial pre-eminence had allowed us to build organizational fat at every level and convince ourselves that it was muscle. Our productivity was growing 2% per year, while in Japan, it was 8-10%. I said that on my watch we would play second fiddle to no one and that with their help and cooperation we would change the way we played the game and win. Happily for us, all our plants were rurally located where the work ethic was alive and well. The challenge was taken up enthusiastically.

We then started a series of exercises involving hundreds of manufacturing employees, initially with the help of outside trainers, who worked competitively to identify manufacturing quality improvement opportunities.

Throughout the company small groups of eight to ten people worked to uncover every conceivable opportunity to improve quality, reduce cost and increase our competitiveness.

## Planning

At the strategic and tactical planning level, we refined our process to make the individual businesses play a larger and more entrepreneurial role. We produced a five-year outlook of our industry, very detailed three-year plans and the usual one-year budget. Corporate management gave the divisional managements more scope to strategize their individual futures so long as it fitted the overall corporate strategy. We delegated more responsibility and authority to divisional management, while retaining firm central control. It was management by participation not by consensus. I warned the Division Managers to be more awed by their new responsibility than excited about their new authority.

## Incentives

Objective performance results were highly incentivized for the top 120 senior managers in the company. Other reward opportunities and equity participation were available to all other employees. These steps fostered ownership and accountability for the individual business strategies and revitalized entrepreneurialism throughout the company.

### A) Short Term Incentives

We modified our annual incentive plan so that the corporate office team earned 75% of its reward from the results of the individual businesses and 25% from the overall company result. The division management teams were working toward earning 75% of their reward for their individual business result and 25% from the overall company result. This encouraged interdependence, so that each of the senior managers had a vested financial interest in helping one another achieve their goals. There were usually four measurements:

| **Performance** | **Focus** |
|---|---|
| Gross Profit | Sales volume, mix, pricing<br>All direct costs |
| Profit Before Tax | All indirect costs |
| Return on Assets | Management of cash, inventory, receivables, and fixed assets |
| Order backlog | Future performance and market share |

**B) Long Term**

Until the second half of the 70s, our management earned its long-term incentive over any four-year period, 80% from four one-year incentive plans and the balance from one four-year measurement of the increase in the value of the stock options held.

We, therefore, introduced a new four-year rolling incentive plan each year, which weighted 60% of the reward to the long-term measurement and 40% to the short. Again, there were four measurements:

| **Performance** | **Focus** |
|---|---|
| EPS Compound Growth | Consistency and predictability |
| New products, programs & customers in $'s of sales | Growth, diversity and new technology |
| Results compared with *Fortune* 1000 | Outperform our industry group |
| Employee productivity | Increase international competitiveness |

The Long Term Incentive Plan awards were a mix of cash and stock.

**Results**

Changing our thinking allowed us to carry out major change in good times, when most managers cannot understand the necessity. ("If it ain't broke, why fix it?") The lowest cost to do anything is to do it correctly the first time. As we did that, quality went up and costs came down. Rework and warranty costs declined, and we operated with less quality inspectors and less inventory. New computer systems were phased in throughout the company. The internal Gold Mine yielded rich veins, which were exploited vigorously to great qualitative and financial advantage.

Between 1976-1982 results improved by the following:

| | |
|---|---|
| Sales | +203% |
| Profits | +310% |
| Productivity | + 58% |
| Return on Assets | + 28% |
| Return on equity | + 80% |
| Market capitalization | +762% |

**Benefits**

- Motivated ownership and accountability by all employees.
- Fostered decentralization of authority and responsibility.
- Generated peer pressure for performance at every level.
- Promoted entrepreneurialism throughout the company.
- Quality improved; costs declined.
- Interdependence was nurtured.
- Shareholders, employees, and customers pleased.

*—Geoff Simmonds*
*Former CEO*
*Simmonds Precision*

# MORE ON MANAGEMENT FROM OTHER MAVERICKS

## What Do You Think?

## Glad You Asked . . .

When I became Secretary of the Army in 1972, the draft was ending and the volunteer Army was new. Its success was in doubt. I knew that it would succeed only with strong support from Congress.

I immediately began a program to convince all the members of Congress of the value of the Army and of our need for their support. While the members and their staffs were always courteous to me, there was a clear undercurrent of hostility based on their belief that the Army and other government institutions would not tell them the truth or at least would not be open with them.

I started a program to open up the Army that became immortalized with "Glad You Asked" bumper stickers that are still in use. The idea was to welcome all questions and give frank answers. This caused quite a stir in an Army that had a reputation of being bureaucratic and uncooperative to outsiders.

The most dramatic, although typical, example of how this policy paid off occurred the day my staff told me that our newly designed helicopter would not fit in the Air Force plane that was to transport it to the battle area. It was a few inches too wide. This was a huge problem. We had spent hundreds of million of dollars on the helicopter's design and had certified its air transportability to Congress. My staff recommended that I tell no one, because they thought we could probably find a solution within six weeks and no one would know.

I rejected that advice and personally visited with the chairmen of the four committees to whom I reported. I informed them of the problem that same day. I said: "The Army has made an unbelievable blunder. It is not high tech to measure the size of a helicopter with a ruler. You have every right to criticize the Army. If you do, you will look good and the Army will look foolish. But if you will give me a few weeks I think we can fix it and I will keep you informed." All four committees gave me the time I asked for. We fixed the problem; there was never any publicity and the Army earned enormous respect form the committees. Imagine what their reaction would have been if they had discovered the problem on their own and realized that I had withheld this information from them.

As the result of an openness and willingness to treat the Congress as a true partner with the Army, I began to get cooperation from the Congress that was unprecedented. The other services never understood why the Army got such favorable treatment.

While this is an Army experience, I have tried to use the "Glad You Asked" policy in every business experience as well. It can be painful, but in the long run, it always works—at least for me.

*—Howard "Bo" Callaway*
*CEO, Callaway Gardens*
*Former Secretary of the Army*

## Avoid Boredom In The Boardroom

You've been there—many times. It's the typical (a.k.a. conventional) inter-company meeting with an agenda that will purportedly cover everything topical from A to Z. Mostly, though, the Zs will emerge—as in ZZZZZZZ (so dreadfully boring that most of the attendees will need strong Italian coffee to avoid falling asleep).

"You all have your agenda sheets in front of you," the moderator will usually intone. "As with most of our weekly/monthly meetings, we'll hear first from Eddie Eyeshade, who'll brief us on profit and loss and the sales and expense trends that he has been tracking since our last meeting. Then we'll ask each department head for a brief report."

As this point, the word STIFLING is an apt barometer of the meeting's mood. If some attendees are still not dozing off when Eyeshade begins his remarks, they will be by the time he concludes. And as for the drone of departmental summations, well, they infuse about as much excitement as the radio rambling of school closing numbers following a snowstorm.

This oft-repeated conventional scenario provides no incentive for creative thought. None of the participants (if you can call them that) has any reason to offer incisive insights. Why muck up everyone's comfort level—not to mention that ever-sacred agenda—by offering comments that will rock the boat?

Such are the thoughts that pervade the brain waves from one end of the room to the other—at a tremendous waste of human resources.

During conventional meetings, the very people who are stationed at critical crossroads in your company's infrastructure—the key employees—are shackled into keeping productive thoughts to themselves. They are muffled, intellectually, by the constraints of a fettering framework. Better they should be given the afternoon off for rest and relaxation than be dragged through the controller's report, the president's homily, the marketing director's slide show, or the executive vice president's summation speech. Ad infinitum, ad nauseam.

Think for a minute, if you will, how much more beneficial an unconventional meeting structure would be to your company's fiscal health.

Start with Step Number One: Tell Eddie Eyeshade to keep himself and his somnolent stats in the back office. Any relevant numbers activity can be put down on paper and distributed well before the meeting commences. Then, if one of your key employees needs clarification (and only then), Eyeshade can be summoned to the meeting to answer questions.

Unconventional Step Number Two, however, is probably even more valuable. It can be stated simply, in four short words: WHAT DO YOU THINK?

Rather than have all those present at your meeting suffer through stilted and cursory reports that are often motivated more by a desire to finish quickly than to provide any meaningful discourse, try the unexpected—the thought provoking.

Take charge of your meeting and can the canned speeches. Let the unconventional in you prepare for the session by studying the responsibilities of all the key attendees. Then, fire the same question at all of them—WHAT DO YOU THINK?

Samples: WHAT DO YOU THINK about how we can save money on XYZ costs? WHAT DO YOU THINK about starting a sales incentive program? WHAT DO YOU THINK of our new flex hours? Etc., etc., etc. Your advanced preparation will help you direct specific information to the proper person and will also help you prod things along if the candid answers are initially slow to appear.

Your goal is to ferret out information that only your key people can be privy to. Opinions of those on the firing line can pay huge benefits. You'll learn more about your business than if you had personally punched a time clock in every corner of every plant or had made hundreds of cold calls from each of your sales districts.

Asking WHAT DO YOU THINK? is akin to debriefing an astronaut who has just returned from the moon. The astronaut's opinions on gravity, for example, have just as much weight, or more, than the opinions of the most celebrated of scholars.

WHAT DO YOU THINK?—four words that can tap untold riches in all forms of competitive advantage. Putting your company first, or keeping it there.

Ask your key employees—and ask them over and over again.

They've been there.

*—Joseph Avenick*
*Author,*
*Business Consultant*

# PART THREE

# Planning

## LRP: Be Flexible, Be Non-Extreme And Just Plain Be There

Winston Churchill was probably well-intentioned when, on behalf of victorious England, he drew chalk lines denoting largely arbitrarily created new nation-states. The new boundaries were more dictated by convenient geography and politics rather than common sense and natural groupings. France, of course, followed along.

"But little did the Allies realize then how they would start a pendulum movement inciting excessive nationalism and rebellious ethnicity. More such largely artificial national groupings later followed such as Yugoslavia, the disputed Alsace-Lorraine, the Baltics, Austria-Hungary," summarizes Duke University's Vice Provost and Professor of Political Science, Dr. Albert Eldridge. "This, of course, followed the divisive precedent of Lord Balfour's earlier establishment of Israel in Palestine."

Eldridge adds: "Virtually all of today's continuing feuding problems of Europe, Eurasia and much of former colonial Africa are rooted in decisions of 77 years ago. Definitely including Bosnia."

Since then the pendulum has swung back and forth with new crises at each apogee: the Weimar Republic, the aborted League of Nations, Chamberlain and Austria hunkering down, Hitler's Third Reich, The Marshall Plan, the European coal community that gave birth to the Common Market. Add to that pendulum swinging the rise of Communism and then its startlingly totally unexpected collapse, along with the Fall of the Berlin Wall.

And, more recently, Europe's 1992 treaty at Maastricht which ended customs, but probably never will achieve a common ECU currency because of nationalism.

## Renewed U.S. Isolationism

Echoing all this in the United States is the Ross Perot anti-NAFTA phenomenon and Pat Buchanan's populist isolationism. In this regard it is worth noting that the relatively inward-looking mood of many in the U.S. today is very similar to that which preceded Pearl Harbor.

History teaches us much about the pendulum of nationalism: (1) usually at only the extreme points were actions initiated and (2) most crises, if not all, were unanticipated. Thus, Long Range Planning (LRP) too far out becomes irrelevant.

Business planning also models itself after similar historical trends as in political science. As for business LRPs, we repeat the observation of J. B. Fuqua, now retired after a long career as one of the very few successful conglomerateurs: "If you have an operational LRP more than 18 months out, burn it."

## Planning Without Plans

So, what to do in business? We suggest to first be flexible. Be ready to innovate, to adjust to new or matured market conditions.

Second, be prepared to adapt to totally unanticipated emerging new events in your field.

Third, don't be uncomfortable about not being "first" to introduce something. Only rarely does it pay to do so. Marconi invented the wireless, forerunner of radio and then TV, in the late 1880s. But radio just kind of lay there until 1912 and the sinking of the Titanic. Then little Bobby Sarnoff's ham radio on Long Island, in touch with the accident, subsequently popularized radio as a belated requirement on all ships.

Facsimile communication was commercially operable in the late 1940s. The *New York Times, Advertising Age* and *Sales Management* magazines started experimenting in a joint venture. But it folded because it took an inefficient three minutes to transmit a single page. It was not until 25 years later, when the Japanese became international players in business markets, that today's practical fax came about. The frustrated Japanese found that Telex could not transmit their oriental letter-characters. So, they reworked facsimile down to 18 seconds a page—and fax finally took off, changing the world forever.

Fourth, try to be neither a hog nor a tail-ender picking up the crumbs. The moderate middle—the 80 percent range between extreme positions—has the best batting average.

Finally, be sure to just plain Be There. Show up. The late great *Life* magazine photographer, Alfred Eisenstaedt, once expressed the secret of his success: "F8 and be there." (F8 is the midway, or point of departure, camera aperture setting.)

Time, Inc.'s, first magazine, *Fortune*, was launched in 1929, one week before the stock market crashed. Henry Luce plunged ahead, anyway. After all, the experts advised the crash could last only as long as a year.

Even just a starting place, and the ability to put up an ante at the table, is the fundamental requirement for all: the biggest or the smallest, the best or the also-rans.

*—August 1995*

## How *Sports Illustrated* Succeeded Despite Its Plan

"The article about Time, Inc's., start-up of *Sports Illustrated* in 1954 was right on . . . with only one major factual error," was the opener of Robert Cowin's letter to me. He was referring to an essay I'd written for *Business Marketing* magazine entitled "Unplanned Events Wreak Havoc on Business Plans."

It described the 13 years and $29 million of losses before *Sports Illustrated* completely reversed its original editorial and business plans and ultimately became one of the most successful magazines in the world. The point was that the original launch plan was to have a sports magazine with a single title ("Sports") aimed at sports participants, not spectators—as is today's successful formula. Mighty *Time's* research and original leaders hadn't thought of swimsuit issues and hadn't a clue on how the National Football League would embrace TV (and the bookmaker-gamblers' interest) creating a new market of watcher-readers, not doers. And the single title had to be abandoned when the research plan belatedly found that McFadden Publishing already owned the "Sport" name. *Time* hated adding the perceived cumbersome "Illustrated," although ironically it would later fit beautifully when the arrival of sports on TV would remake *Sports Illustrated*.

Cowin is an authority about *Time's* palmier days, before Steve Ross, Gerald Levine and Time-Warner. In the 50s and 60s Cowin was a key Time, Inc., executive and corporate circulation director for its stable of the top magazines of the era: *Life, Fortune, Time* and then *Sports Illustrated*. (This was before the days of today's single-titled *Money* and *People*.)

"The Time executives did not agree to the sports magazine idea 'within 60 seconds' as reported in *USA Today*," continues Cowin. "They did only after Henry R. Luce (HRL) finally made up his mind. As a matter of fact there was a great debate for two years—and a lot of other new magazine ideas were considered. The leaders were a highly sophisticated *Atlantic Monthly* literary type—and what really scared hell out of the editors—a women's magazine that HRL spouse Claire Booth was urging. The last thing the editors wanted was Claire in the picture."

Cowin also clarified the origins of the enormously successful annual swimsuit special issue. Confirming that indeed it was never in the original plan, he recalled that a junior editor had an idea that "a Caribbean resort story in January might attract some advertisers like Jantzen, and resorts might pump up some extra advertising in this anemic ad month."

Now, personally, as a dedicated sports participant, I always enjoyed the original *SI*, and haven't read the current spectator-orientated format in years. But, considering its earlier floundering, it's amazing it survived those earlier days. Cowin recalls the chaos:

"HRL first appointed Ernie Havemann to be *Sports Illustrated's* managing editor. Ernie accepted and then within two weeks wrote a most profound long memo stating why he had to decline. So Luce tapped Sid James, a junior editor from *Life*, but not a sportsman. *Life's* ad director, Harry Phillips, was picked as publisher, but knew nothing about any aspect of publishing except Madison Avenue. I got the circulation job with no contest.

"So here we had an editor who knew next to nothing about the subject matter and a publisher who wasn't the least bit interested in learning anything about circulation, production, promotion, magazine finance, etc.

"Only Time, Inc., could get away with this," Cowin continues. But they didn't get away with such inept leadership and the magazine floundered for lack of purpose and direction. Powerful factions formed throughout the company at every level.

"Roy Larson encouraged the editing for the elite, or as you put it . . . the participant sportsmen. For example, 'How to Cook Rock Shrimp on the Fantail of a Schooner in Nantucket Sound,'" Cowin recalls. "But finally after several soul searching years of questioning, HRL brought in Andre Laguerre . . . a cigar-chomping Frenchman who was Time's bureau chief in Europe . . . but a devoted sportsman. In a few years it began to turn toward the magazine it is now, with color, humor and flash.

"You were right, John, in noting that this direction dovetailed with the early explosion of sports on TV. I always thought it ironic that TV killed *Life,* but made *Sports Illustrated.*"

Cowin takes a deep breath, then sums up: "Talk about going from the frying pan into the fire. For me, as the continuing circulation director, it was hell. I lived through five publishers, six ad directors, and an assortment of promotion directors and general and business managers. In addition, because The Business Plan never worked, all of us with *SI* were practically ostracized from the rest of the company hierarchy for dragging down profit sharing."

Moral: If you're going to start a new magazine, be prepared to abandon the original plan.

*—May 1994*

## Should Every Business Have A Skunk Works?

"How A Skunk Works Kept Mustang Alive" was the unusual headline that jumped at me from the *Wall Street Journal* front page. The story narrated Ford's revival of their former famous Mustang car line.

Skunk Works. Intriguing name. The last time I heard it used was three years ago at Ocean Reef Club when several fellow retirees were sharing former business and marketing tales. Two had been top executives at Midland; Michigan's Dow Chemical. Cautiously, even today, they tip-toe talked a little about Dow's skunk works of the past years. They suspected, but didn't know for sure, that others, most certainly some of their competitors, had similar operations.

Oversimplified, as I understood it, there are times when a breakthrough crash course on immediate research or products is perceived as needed. Secrecy is imperative. The company's regular bureaucracy has to be by-passed. So a handful or two of chemists, engineers and manufacturing employees are recruited, relieved from their normal responsibilities, provided funds and isolated at working facilities to "go find what can be found . . . and then do it."

All of this has to be covered by a credible "cover" from mainstream colleagues both in the business and outside. It can get complicated: sudden resignations and absence from industry committees and conference activities have to be rationalized. Indeed, in most cases, a skunk works operation has to be "off the books." Often not even a board member (well, sometimes maybe one is sworn to secrecy) knows of its existence. Creative accounting masks it from the balance sheet, operating statement and pesky business analysts.

An irony is that often to the degree a skunk works operation can continue successfully, in order not to blow their cover the unit cannot "come in from the cold" and take open credit.

**Skunk Works Origination**

Curious about how skunk works got started in marketing and business, I started tracking it down. It appears that the original skunk works manager was Kelly Johnson, who is still a legend at Lockheed Corporation. In 1943 he organized the first gang that was charged by the Pentagon to have Lockheed develop quickly, quietly, efficiently, a new class of World War II fighter plane. The very successful F-80 was the result.

Subsequently, the Lockheed skunk works style was also responsible for such as the famous U-2 spy plane. And in the late 1970s the plane that did so well in the Gulf War, stealth fighter F-117, was similarly developed by Lockheed. Indeed, Lockheed says they have registered the name "Skunk Works."

Johnson's fundamentals were predicated upon "25 to 30 key people working with a select few in the military." The challenge was "how do you empower program management—keeping it out of the normal bureaucratic chain?" And, key, "how do you shield it from internal resentment, interference as well as the enemy (or business and marketing competitors)?" Johnson developed *Fourteen Skunk Works Guidelines*, which Lockheed willingly shares. But don't ask them about the shadowy Aurora spy plane, America's successor to the SR-71. Officially it doesn't exist.

*—September 1993*

## Planning? Often It's Better Just To Wing It

Okay, student executives-to-be, the formula is "Plan your work . . . and then work your plan." That has always been one of the primary B-school "buzzwords," It sounds good, but let's take a look at the record.

We can start with the daddy of all plans, The Marshall Plan. Even it didn't foresee the implications of refinancing former enemies with the latest modern tools and equipment (so that they could compete and then beat us in world markets).

Admittedly, some very general planning objectives are still operable, like the basics: plan to make a profit; define and redefine your market; and establish your reputation for quality, honesty, and financial accountability. But, beyond that, it's mostly the unplanned and the unforeseen that really count: luck, timing, unanticipated new markets, and personalities (individuals do make a difference).

Just look back during the past 10 or 20 years in any field of your choice. Then ask yourself how the status today of that activity differs from the planned expectations of a decade or so ago. Any "unplanned impact" list would include such as: computers, cable TV, the Berlin Wall, Star Wars, Communism's Evil Empire, Arkansas politicians, or the NASA shuttle trips to the moon.

How about the 'sophisticated think-tank computer models, you ask? Well, consider that when the Arabs instituted their 1970s oil embargo, not one model had cranked in that alternative scenario. Not Wharton, IBM, Rand, M.I.T, nor Chase (according to then Conference Board economist Al 'Red" Sommers), All models had to be scrapped—and started over.

Remember, success . . . and often failure . . . come in spite of planning.

*—March 1996*

## Forecasting The Economy? Ask Your Doctor

Seeing again Dr. Edward Felder and his wife, Judy, I was reminded of an unconventional method of market forecasting. Ed's still an extremely knowledgeable internist of the old school (house calls, cares about the patient). But his business instincts were sharpened when bad eyes forced him into a very successful Fairfield County consulting second career with companies such as Union Carbide.

Inevitably, we got to discussing the current recession, Particularly in New York and Northeast areas. Who, among the "experts" do you believe has The Word? What Should a company's current marketing plan be? Why are the economists mostly so wrong?

That last question really bugs me. With all the computers and think-tanks, why don't they have a better track record? For 30 years my company produced the interim census—the Surveys of Buying Power. Therefore I know all the official government excuses on time lags and endless readjusting. And I'm very familiar with "expert" forecasters and their wriggling excuses: "On the other hand . . ." and "I was too right. but some unanticipated factors were introduced . . . ."

Some say that a rise in luxury sales is a leading indicator. But believe me, you can be fooled on that one. In the almost cashless economy of the current Northeast, professionals such as doctors and lawyers, normally good upscale buyers, find the easy way to get a malpractice suit is to press on collecting their bills. During these times, a new Lexus, Mercedes or Cadillac will muck up their image of need.

"You've forgotten what I told you 25 years ago, when I was still in patient practice," noted the good doctor Felder. "It's really simple. I always had an instant handle on whether or not we were in better times, lousier times or more of the same."

"Ed, the memory is the second thing to go. (And so I've

forgotten the first!) Tell me again," I pleaded.

"My Darien and New Caanan patients were mostly middle and upper-middle-class mainstream middle Americans, wives of business executives who led the way in the economy's ups and downs," Felder replied. "Their elective cosmetic surgery interest was a never-failing barometer of the times. If they wanted a mole removed, or a chin-lift, you knew things were headed up. Otherwise it was flat—or worse."

Now, think-tanks, how can you put that in a computer?

*—July 1991*

## A Dozen Mistakes You Can Make Selling Your Company

"So you think you can afford to sell the company . . . and maintain your standard of living? I don't." Morgan Browne so cautioned me in a memo back in 1987. Browne was my chief operating officer and himself an 8% stockholder in the company, Bill Communications.

At the time I owned 60% of the stock. An ESOP I had set up in 1975 owned 20%. The remainder was in the hands of about 25 employees.

Browne's caution sparked my personal review, periodically shared with the directors, of our alternatives. Simplified, they were: sell now, sell later, go public, do nothing. Seven months from Browne's memo, almost to the day, I made the agonizing decision to sell. Now.

My choice narrowed down to my desire to resolve, as much as possible, the company's welfare during my lifetime (I was then age 66), rather than to leave it to chance after my death. I wanted to pick the buyer, rather than have it picked for us. The financial motivation was secondary, as Browne's caution had proved right. On balance, I was better off not selling.

But in researching my decision, research that continues to this day and includes more than 70 executives who have participated in the sale of their companies, I have developed this list of 12 mistakes:

**1. You will have total control of the situation.**

If you are in a buyer's market . . . or a tough sale, forget it. You are going to be jerked around. A lot. And don't expect each concession you make to be the last one asked or demanded. They'll keep coming, the next day after you've given in on the last one.

**2. You will be given credit for prudent, low or zero debt financial management.**

To the contrary. In today's debt-driven financial world, more likely there will be repressed sneers and disrespect for not fully "working your assets." The fad today is strictly cash flow.

**3. A buyer is a buyer is a buyer . . . no matter who, the best sales price will be the same.**

This will be the perspective of your investment banker or broker, whose cut is an up-front, off-the-top percentage . . . regardless of how it is constructed. It makes little difference to them if it is all cash, paper, staggered payment, ballooned or whatever. But for you the seller (and your buyer as well), there are substantial advantages and disadvantages between different types of buyers, and how the sale is constructed.

**4. Your exit-contract benefits can be the same with any type of buyer.**

No way. You can have, without undue pain for the buyer, substantially greater perks if it is an established operating company. They simply tax-deduct "expense" it over time. But a leveraged venture company is under great pressure to wring out maximum profits. They want to look good to their lending syndicate to set a good tone for the next deal.

**5. You will get substantial extra multiples for your prestige property or top-of-market positioning.**

Well, maybe some. And you will attract a wider number of interested buyers. But when you get down to the short strokes, that all falls away. It all comes down to cash flow; the rest is all schmooze and talk.

**6. You will be remembered/recognized by many in the company two years after the sale.**

In many instances it won't take even six months before your call to a former comrade at the office will be met by: "May I tell him who you are with?" Or, "Is there anything I can handle for you, instead?" Your degradation will be compounded if your buyer has sold off divisions and made sweeping executive changes. Be prepared to explain who you are, from scratch.

**7. The perception and priorities of your former associates toward you will remain pretty much the same.**

After all, a business lifetime of working together! Sorry, with few exceptions, it just isn't the way it works out.

YOU: "Hi, Joan, how are things? Is Charlie there?"

JOAN (interrupting—or after an interminable pause): "Can he get back to you later?"

**8. Your advice will continue to be sought by your former business colleagues.**

Well, for a while some will go through the motions with polite lip service on "consultation. But, in reality, it will be mostly informing you after the fact of the decision. Your carbon copies become "FYI" . . . and even these will fast fade. Could it be that some acquirers feel that to ask for help from former executives would be interpreted as a sign of weakness to their investors or remaining managers?

**9. Your phone will ring off the hook with outside offers of consulting opportunities, now that you have the time and availability.**

With some inevitable exceptions (but mostly in the non-compensation pro bono public areas), it just won't happen. The phone calls, luncheon invitations ("Why don't we just get together and talk!"), head-table philanthropic appeals, requests to go on boards, former contacts looking for an angle or an "in". . . all start drying up to a trickle.

**10. Continuing stockholders and employees will recognize and give you credit for your past paternal efforts.**

Alas, very few will. But there will be a few rewarding exceptions, from old-timers and newcomers.

**11. Making your own plane reservations is a "piece of cake."**

While not the most vital, this has to be the most traumatic change, according to our survey of departed executives . . . and their spouses!

**12. Failure to "dress" the company for sale.**

Planning for the sale at least a year ahead is very desirable, if at all possible. Early retirements can be implemented, plow-back reinvestments can be tightened, offices and departments can be consolidated, new starts or acquisitions can be deferred, profit incentives can be stepped up.

**13. (You're getting a baker's dozen of mistakes.) If you had to do it over again, you wouldn't sell.**

True, the selling process has its wrenching aspects. But it is equally sure that the time comes when you realize that "if you go" is no longer operative. The real word is "when" you go. The time to sell is when it becomes clear it is the best of all the varyingly unattractive alternatives. So, take the money and walk (don't run) to the next fun exit . . . adventure. Now, maybe for the first time since college days, you can indulge in time and leisure. Fulfill travel dreams, dive into charitable make-a-difference projects. You can even write a book about "How To Sell A Company."

*—February 1990*

## Once You Succeed Unconventionally, Stay Unconventional

Remember "Walkin' Lawton"? Lawton Chiles first got himself overwhelmingly elected as U.S. Senator from Florida by literally (unconventionally) putting on his walking shoes and going out to meet the public. He asked: "What do you want? What are your concerns?"

He did it again in a successful populist campaign for Governor of Florida. But, after winning, he put his shoes in the closet, closed his ears and switched to an authoritarian style ("Do As I Say, I Know Best"). The *Miami Herald* did a report card on Chiles, saying his fall from grace has earned him worse marks than his perpetually embattled predecessor, Bob Martinez (even at Martinez's nadir).

**Does Only Management Know Best?**

This is "Decade-Time." You know: Where-We've-Been in the 1980s and Where-We're-Going in the 1990s. Summaries and forecasts are swamping us. We've been awash in reviews and predictions.

"Gorby," The Man of the Decade. Runner-up events: Default of Communism, U.S. switching from credit to debt society, Wall Street greed, drugs, AIDS, Reagan, Japan's growth, the homeless.

So far, no media voice has fingered the one worldwide dominant theme of the 80s and probable watchword for the 90s: The decline and fall of Authoritarianism. It is being challenged or routed everywhere, in every country, sector or discipline. Russia started it rolling (will Perestroika become a brand name of a new vodka in their move toward capitalism?). Then Poland, now all of Eastern Europe and China (temporarily aborted, but still most latent). De-authoritarianism is affecting parts of organized religion, including the mighty Roman Catholic Church, whose practitioners are not now as catholic in following the Pope on everything. Certainly the diminishment of some strident TV evangelists is another example.

No sector seems immune to de-authoritarianism. Take Big Business. Contents pages of *Forbes, Business Marketing, Business Week* and *Fortune* magazines continue to chronicle how autocratic management has fallen out of bed. *Fortune's* annual "Most Autocratic Managers" issue viewed with caution the future business success of most of those they featured. In a recent story on "The Trust Gap" (between managers and employees), it is noted that "Organizations audit their financial resources, but fail to take the temperature of their own employees."

Why? "Because asking underlings questions has been tantamount to letting them run the show. Later, not listened to, employees return the compliment. Missives are read with disbelief by everybody below the level of VP.

The auto industry continues to provide examples of both change (Japan's successful Participative Management) and being kind of grudgingly backed into change (GM and Chrysler; Ford has changed further, faster, so far). The Germans, with their Teutonic engineers, seem stalled as an exception somewhere in the middle. But, all are finding "authoritarianism" is not at all the same as "authority." Instead, the most effective authority and power now flows from bottom up, rarely from top down.

As business gets tougher, smarter, more competitive—domestically and internationally—survival management is junking the former "Here's your Job Description . . . just do it" mode. More are adopting the credo of Ren McPherson when he was head of Dana Corp. and later Dean of Stanford's Graduate School Of Business. As summarized in *In Search of Excellence,* McPherson advocates practicing what he finds are the Four Most Important Words In Business: "What Do You Think?"

### U.S. Management Coming Back

There are, fortunately, many signs of a turnaround in imaginative, entrepreneurial management making inroads among even the rigid giants. Ocean Reef homeowner Dave Dort has just written us a thoughtful letter from his other home at Flint, Michigan (keystone location of the much maligned General Motors). Commenting on GM changes, Dort writes: "What's beginning to happen at GM gives heart for the country. As always, the people who are making (new) history are unconscious of it (the flak and brickbats), because they are too busy." Dort notes that Flint's Buick manufacturing operation has risen from the depths to where this year it is recognized as the highest quality assembly plant in America (second best in the world). He adds: "A new young executive coming fresh has turned-around a struggling A.C. Spark Plug division to the point where this GM division is now selling also to the Japanese and European automakers." When this young exec took over, key among his style armament was a variation of "What Do You Think?"

De-authoritarianism is even hitting our hospitals. Ever been a patient, employee or volunteer in a hospital? It used to be strictly "by the numbers management." Nurses, who are always closest to and most with the patients, have been traditionally almost roboted in their responsibilities. Historically, their common sense screams for justice have been summarily ignored. Few initiatives nor judgments could be taken if not pre-ordained by hospital MANAGEMENT. One result has been a flight of frustrated quality nurses from hospitals into private practice.

Texas' famous Heartland Hospital has turned all that around. Now, management is listening to and fully involving nurses in all possible deliberations and decisions. The nurses are coming back to the hospital.

During the 80s, mid-sized businesses ($10 to $900 million sales annually) moved into leadership in flexibility, innovation, growth and international competitiveness. In all but a few cases, mid-sized businesses are far less autocratic, more open and participative in decision making. The result, increasingly more of the *Fortune* 500 today seek every way to emulate the less rigid mid-sized competitor/supplier. They downsize, establish and help finance "entrepreneurial boutiques," try everything to become less autocratic—more quickly adaptive.

Responding to this, Duke University's Graduate School of Business (Fuqua) has set up a first-ever Mid-Sized Business Research Educational Center. Although Duke will become the research "core," education coordination will be expanding beyond Duke's Research Triangle. Widespread but selective affiliations are being sought. Already cooperating are organizations like the Young Presidents' Organization, World Business Council, American Business Conference, and Chief Executives Organization. Contacts at universities like Stanford, Colgate, and the University of Western Ontario are following developments closely.

Of course, there are times when it's go or no go. Down to one man's decision. Like the time Lincoln was outvoted eight-to-one at a Cabinet meeting, and Lincoln said: "The Ayes have it, because I am the Aye."

Still, de-authoritarianism should continue to be one of the key trends of the 90s. It may spell all but the end of "Big Daddy Knows Best."

What Do You Think?

*—December 1991*

# VIEWPOINTS FROM OTHER MAVERICKS

# Planning

## Training Does *Not* Cost Money

One of the most fundamental principles I learned as a young man was from reading the autobiography of Bernard Baruch. A key thought that came through his autobiography was to be a counterintuitive thinker. If the crowd were going one way, maybe he should go the other. That would be a natural principle to a Wall Street man as was Baruch, but he used it far more prolifically in areas other than just in the trading of stocks and bonds. I've used it as a benchmarking process to great advantage.

The Motorola story in Japan is looked upon by at least the Japanese and some Americans as being a bit maverick. The conventional wisdom was that one shouldn't press hard. One should just let trade develop in whatever is the natural way. We recognize that whereas we had to be gracious and appropriately deferential in Japan, we also had to use power. We had to use power to overcome a very important principle that influences strategies. That principle is the principle of sanctuary. You can't let your competitor have a sanctuary. We had to use all manner of legitimate power to force open the Japanese market so that the Japanese could not retain the sanctuary they had created for themselves.

About 15 years ago, when musing over the fundamental issue of how to be competitive, I finally concluded that I was competitive in sports to different levels of success depending on how much better the other person was trained. I derived from that the simple principle that for our company to be competitive, we had to be competitive, counterpart to counterpart, not in some general corpus body evaluation. My associates agreed with me that there were smarter chief executive officers in our industry, and we had to acknowledge that it would be hard to us to be competitive if I couldn't stand up to their performance. In turn, they had to stand up to the performance of the best in their field, etc. But when it came to resourcing, my associates said we're going to have to find a way of educating by spending very little time and very little money. At which point I concluded the principle of training doesn't cost and that we were going to allocate resources but gain so much more from the allocation of resources that we would be the beneficiary and eventually the winner. That was an unaccepted idea by everyone in its initial proposals.

*—Bob Galvin*
*Chairman of the*
*Executive Committee*
*Motorola Corp.*

## Buying and Building Companies

I can't really say that I can remember any maverick experiences except when I met a member of the Young Presidents Organization (YPO) from Ireland. I was in Monaco on my way to Dublin to investigate starting a factory in that city, and I ended up building a plant with the YPOer as a partner. The maverick part might be that there was only one box company in Dublin, and when they found out I was starting a plant, they told me they would drive me into bankruptcy. My reply was: "Be my guest." I ended up starting the plant in Dublin, and ultimately was bought out by that company—not only in Ireland but in the U.S. as well.

As a 28-year-old, I went to a YPO seminar in Los Angeles. There were 12 people at the "How to Buy Companies Through Leverage" session. The seminar was headed by Bob Hansberger and Nick Slago. As a result of that seminar, I ended up buying 12 companies, merging them, and going public in 1970. I always say that YPO helped me more than I care to admit.

*—Don J. Hindman*
*Chairman*
*Clark Foodservice, Inc.*

## Strategic Planning Is Too Slow For Today

The first move in any company is to eliminate strategic planning functions. Any effort in that area will make your company too inflexible to deal with today's fast moving world.

No one can predict what sort of business life will be created by the Internet. But you can predict that a lot of large companies will be mortally wounded by these upstarts in ten years.

No matter how successful you become, you must fight cost every day. You do that by keeping the "fear of failure" culture alive and well after the reality of failure is gone.

*—Walter Forbes*
*Chairman*
*CUC International*

## Goals, Goals, Goals

I am a very goal-oriented person. In my early twenties, when I first began my business career, I took a very small card and wrote down my personal and business goals. I continued to update the list for many, many years. I kept this list in two places. One was in my wallet, which at the time had a plastic sleeve and on the front sheet of the sleeve appeared my card with my goals. The second card was located on my mirror in my bathroom. Each time I shaved in the morning, I looked at that list and knew why I got up and went to work. Every time I opened up my wallet I saw that list. This constantly kept my goals keenly focused in my mind.

Even in the last few years as we went through the "great Ocean Reef adventure," I kept the goals that related to that endeavor clearly detailed in writing on my desk here at Ocean Reef. I have found my road to success was to clearly know exactly where I was going.

*—Alan Goldstein*
*Past Chairman*
*Ocean Reef Club*

## Breakthrough Leadership

My experience has been that it isn't the five percent variances that make for great rewards. Rather, great rewards come from dramatic revolutionary changes and not just evolutionary fine tuning.

I will share one experience that makes my point. For a number of years I have been managing a privately held mutual fund. If you are going to make money in that business on a consistent basis, you must constantly look in the rear view mirror to analyze what you do that works and what doesn't. Putting aside my strategies and the fundamentals of the businesses invested in, there were two variables involved in all the really big winners. There was dramatic and continual change taking place in those businesses, and they had real leaders running those businesses—not just caretakers. The leaders were identifiable in that they were making it happen . . . turning new ideas into commercially viable products and processes.

I don't remember the order of things and it really doesn't matter—but I put a bunch of ingredients together into a mental stew. Among these were: I needed to get to company CEOs in a way that they would discuss how their businesses were innovating. I put a tag on this process: Breakthrough Leadership (BtL). I started including references to this concept in speeches I gave. I realized other CEOs would be interested in this BtL process.

The result: I now produce a monthly audio newsletter of interviews I do with CEOs and top business thinkers on how they discover new ways of doing things and how them make it happen. It has been very successful. I am investing in BtL companies in the Link Fund and making a pot full. Lastly, and most importantly, it's fun.

*—Jack Linkletter*
*Lecturer, consultant*

# PART FOUR

# Sales & Marketing

## Sometimes It Pays To Turn Problem Upside Down

Looking at the announcements of the newly restyled Caddys, I'm reminded of one of my favorite sales-research stories. In the world of marketing and advertising, decision-making is a constant. Maybe more than any other business. At least the practitioners are vocal and sometimes amusing about the "art."

"I know my advertising is effective 50% of the time," noted one famous marketing pioneer during the 1920s. "The problem is I don't know which half it is," he lamented.

Remember the high-styling emphasis of automobile tail-fins? Introduced by Cadillac, for a decade thereafter they swept the industry. The following story of how the tail-fins came about is not entirely apocryphal.

After World War II, General Motors started switching its thinking from war-time production to customer-oriented marketing. The charge: find out what they want . . . then give it to them. But how?

For years, much market research had been based upon house-to-house canvassing with long questionnaires on preferences and dislikes. GM's principal advertising agency, Campbell Ewald, had been given the stylish tail-fin idea as a future option question. Their first returns were highly negative in answer to questions like: "Is styling important to your car purchase decision? Would you buy anything that had, say, rising tail-fins?"

"No. No way."

Most polled insisted that they were only interested in what would be perceived as virtuous features such as value and safety.

**Turn Question Around**

Then some unsung pollster had an idea. This time when they knocked on doors, after finishing the standard questions, they added such as:

"Now, tell us, please. How do you think your neighbor rates styling? Would he like tail-fins?"

"Oh, yeah, he's big on impressions. Sure, he'd love tail-fins!"

The next decade of tail-fins growing bigger and bigger is history. It also caused a lot of poll-taking and business market research changes.

All this is a bit humbling, of course. But then so is a paraphrase of another enduring marketing wisdom that also came out of the 1920s: "I've learned that about the time I get weary and bored with my advertising copy . . . just leave it alone. Chances are it is only now beginning to be effective."

*—September 1991*

## A Better Maverick Way To Contact The 'Mr. Bigs'

A conventional wisdom in sales and marketing is: "The cat that makes many calls gets more kittens." Or: "You gotta know the territory." And: "From 9 until 5, plan your work and work your plan."

These kind of homilies are nice if your desire is to be only average. But it's that last "9 until 5" that I want to address. To be superior, not just average, you have to gear up differently. Be a slight maverick . . . that is, don't just follow the pack. This is particularly true the higher up, more important and difficult to access the sales or advertising target.

A test. First, put yourself in your target's shoes. If he's made it to the top, and wants to stay there, one sure reason is because he's geared his own "9 until 5" personal contacts to *his* customers. Right? So, then, when does he have time to think, create, not be on the go?

Hah! The secret is one I guarantee for most all. Be resourceful and ferret out his direct telephone line, the one that by-passes the switchboard. Then place your call to him either before 9:00 a.m. or after 5:15 p.m. Only.

Or, better still, try him on a Saturday or Sunday. Either way you'll have a great chance of finding him/her . . . and without distraction. Because they may have risen to the top with similar maverick approaches, chances are you will be admired, not resented, for your resourcefulness.

One concluding caveat: Make those off-hour telephone calls *only to your target's office phone*. And my wife reminds me to caution on never, ever phoning to your target's home. You lose the spouse's approval, and your target may not welcome being awakened from a nap.

*—January 1996*

## Get'em To Lean Toward You

What was your first sales job? I was reminded of mine the other day—it was selling the late *Colliers* magazine house-to-house. With door-to-door direct selling all but gone today, I wonder if our kids are getting the basic selling lessons we earned 40 or 50 years ago.

First, let me share how this reflection came about. At Ocean Reef (my winter home in the Florida Keys), only about 670 acres encompass the entire community's 1,500 residences. When you mail a letter to a neighbor, however, it can take longer to get there than one you mail from Miami to San Francisco. Because of this, Ocean Reefers often bypass the postal service and leave messages on their neighbors' car windshields or front doors.

Well, one time I went further and rang a doorbell. The lady of the house opened the front door and cautiously peered around it. Instinctively, I took one large step backward. Then, she realized I was no threat. Visibly relaxed, she leaned forward and receptively cocked one ear. Whether she realized it or not, I now had her attention.

Suddenly, it all came back. It was just as my *Colliers* district route manager had instructed us 50 years ago on how to open your sales story—get the prospect to lean toward you.

I checked all this out with Nat Zivin, an Ocean Reef neighbor and retired president of the Fuller Brush Co., the one-time king of direct sales.

Nat's first job in the Great Depression was also selling *Colliers*; he would start at the top floor of a Chicago skyscraper and work his way down with the same opening: "Please let me have two minutes of your time." A selling style all but gone now, but let Nat tell it:

"In the old days our best salesmen often became treasured family friends. Their route returns would be welcomed by housewives who would put on the coffee and pour out problems they wouldn't think of laying on their husbands and priests. All salesmen need a good ear, and our best were great listeners."

*Colliers, Liberty, American,* and the like are now long gone. So are the original versions of *Life* and *The Saturday Evening Post.* A very different Fuller Brush still lives, now owned by Sara Lee. The sales force is almost all female. The primary sales method is telephone and Avon-like parties. Not much is expected of a very modest retail store in a test market. Only in very small towns is there a remnant of door-to-door. (In the larger cities, peepholes, triple latches, electronic sirens, and guard dogs are the rule these days.)

The behavioral sciences have come a long way in marketing since those ground-breaking days. The dictionaries didn't even know it was supposed to be a (gasp!) science. Focus groups, T (training) groups, the Grid, and quality circles are all great, but I hope it's not at the sacrifice of the basics we learned years ago. In today's sales arena, an old-fashioned approach would be refreshingly unconventional.

*—December 1991*

## How Conventional Businesses Are Changing— Selective Is Better Than Bigger

Remember the days in the 1970s of large conglomerates being developed with almost totally unrelated businesses? Few lasted. Unsuccessful, they continue to be broken up, sold by the piece, usually less than for what was paid.

Then came the 1980s with junk-bonded Leveraged Buyouts (LBOs). They suffered the same fate.

Conglomerates and LBOs had in common the objective of piling on growth upon growth. The bigger the better. That's "out" now. Replacing it is what is called "Target Marketing." That is . . . "selective rather than bigger, qualitative less is better than mass." The business aim now is to hit 29 singles, rather than go for one home run every ten times at bat.

Magazines reflect this trend. Business publication Standard Rate & Data Service (SRDS) lists 5,000 separate magazines (from *ABA Banking Journal* to *Your Church*); the consumer SRDS details 1,700 different magazine titles. Broadcast media, particularly network television, will have a tougher time adjusting. Already the unconventional, highly selective cable programming that offers 28 smaller slices of more targeted audiences makes the future of the Big Three TV networks questionable. The weekly newspaper increases as the major new force in reaching, via newsprint, selective readers with specially targeted editorial content. Conventional afternoon dailies, with a diffuse circulation, have all but expired, partly because of this. The morning and Sunday papers continue to make major adjustments.

### Airlines And The Bigger Size Trap

The airline story is likewise illustrative. First Pan Am tumbled from leadership by acquiring and mangling National. Continental grabbed, merged, then folded sparky upstart

People. Pan Am made matters worse by acquiring Air Florida. (Some argue its worst acquisition was the hiring of Air Florida's CEO as Pan Am's own.) Texas Air unfriendlied Eastern. Republic was swallowed by Northwest. More recently, USAir has been trying to digest Piedmont. In fairness, conversely and to USAir's credit, they run counter to Bigness by serving markets the Bigs don't want.

Evidence continues to mount that acquisition-growth of this kind—with the primary emphasis on quick short-term profits or stock plays—gratefully may at last become a management practice dodo bird, an idea whose time has gone.

As for hostile acquisitions (even in academia), takeover mouthpieces, like Harvard Business School's Michael Jensen, seem increasingly discredited, if only for revelations of lack of objectivity. "At Pennsylvania anti-takeover legislative hearings, Jensen signed a petition on behalf of the now infamous Belzberg company's then attempted takeover of Armstrong. He did this without disclosing his 50,000 stock appreciation rights. The law passed, but, in apparent gratitude, Belzberg rewarded Jensen with a board seat." (Excerpted from *Unfriendly Takeovers,* William A. Sax, Executive-in-Residence, Fuqua School of Business, Duke University.)

To document, let's examine a few industries. First, continue with the airlines. Five of the above-mentioned acquisitions (forget that polite euphemism "mergers") were cases of whales swallowing fish. The other, Texas' hostile takeover of Eastern, was a junk-bonded minnow trapping the big fish. In all cases there was a common bond of impatience with natural growth. The impetus was on getting much bigger—right now. The aim was to woo short-term Wall Street traders. (I repeat: traders, not investors.) Other factors like plant equipment, employees, community, customers, markets, and longer term growth compatibilities were subordinated.

Aye. As in *Hamlet,* "there may lie the rub." Mergers and Acquisitions (M&A) today are just not what they used to be. A case can be made that they haven't been, with some exceptions, since the Depression years.

## The Get Bigger Boom

Historically, M&A became bigger and more complex than cutting off your neighbor's water route, then buying his land and livestock at a bargain. "Get Bigger" took giant steps when Henry Ford perfected an assembly line for his single Model T product. His revolutionary $5 per day minimum wage made it sensible to add production volume (more shifts) to machinery just waiting to be utilized.

Then Alfred P. Sloan, Jr., father of General Motors, invented a new wrinkle in production and marketing; mass niches. (No, not an oxymoron.) But he centralized staff functions to cut costs. Sloan's genius invented the major target selling to five overlapping but distinctive economic classes: Chevy, Pontiac, Buick, Olds and Cadillac. Customers "graduated" with age and increased disposable income.

Today, in the auto industry, Bigness is a problem, Ford and GM first spawn and test their new models for the states for a couple of years via their smaller European subsidiaries. Acquired "bigness" can backfire. Today Chrysler has all but dissolved its recent acquisition of Renault. Ironically, the almost incidental by-product of the Renault acquisition—Jeep—remains successful because of its selective niche position.

## Others Downsize

Federated Department Store's bigness acquisition binge resulted in bankruptcy. Belatedly they are trying to sell off stores, get smaller. Donald Trump's bigger fiascos seem headed toward having the Donald return to the shelter of his father's financial support. Beatrice Foods' over-conglomeration is still being broken up. The jury remains out on many with ego-trip overtones, such as RJR Nabisco.

At some time, certainly after World War II, too much size for many started being counterproductive. They lost flexibility, became prisoners of what they had to work with. Many companies, still proceeding as before, have as yet to realize this, unable to reverse field. During the last 40 years, the acquisition game switched away from being one that was relatively strategic and market-oriented.

Indeed, we suggest, the "M&A Game" gradually crept into becoming largely corporate ego-driven. Upon climbing the company musical chairs to become, at last, CEO —at age 60—Mr. Nouveau Boss realized he had only five years until mandatory retirement to "make his mark for history." How? Quickly now: "Grow fast. Acquire." This gobble-up growth drive is of course further spurred by Wall Street trader (again, not investor) pressure for short-term, force-fed, temporary quarterly results.

In sum: let growth be as natural as possible. If acquiring, make it as related as possible. Some say that absorbing growth of any kind over 15 percent per year creates problems not worth the risk.

Don't necessarily think small. Instead, think "selectively."

*—December 1995*

# Keep All The Acquisition Boys Away From L. L. Bean

In the fall of 1945, I penciled an outline of my right foot on a sheet of paper and started my personal love affair with L. L. Bean. Shortly thereafter, my first pair of "customized" Bean Maine hunting boots came in the mail. The boots were fine, but I had a problem with the size of a separate item I had ordered. However, by phone, founder Leon Bean personally straightened it out.

For generations, this Freeport, Maine company has been one of America's national treasures, a model of the customer-is-in-the-driver's-seat sales and marketing. If Bean was public, and not a closely held family company, you can just picture today's corporate raiders salivating over the short-term lean-and-mean profits they could squeeze out. It would be quick curtains for Bean's lifelong advertised policy: "If you're not satisfied for any reason, we will return your money."

**'Good Hunting'**

Nor would takeover boys indulge other Bean practices.

A few years ago, for instance, an old friend invited me to a quail shoot at his company's Majik Plantation.

At the last minute, I discovered my Bean boots were tattered beyond repair. A panicky weekend call to Freeport. But how to be sure I would get the right size? At the time, Bean's only facsimile machine was in a different office.

"Not to worry," replied Bean's representative, assuring me I wouldn't have to make a personal Sunday call to their president. "We'll express you two sizes. You return the unused pair."

"Visa, MasterCard, or American Express?" I asked.

"None of the above," she replied. "We'll re-bill you after you get straightened out. Good hunting."

Beautiful. And uniquely American selling.

Please don't let L. L. Bean go public and risk being acquired.

*—January 1992*

## How Tennis Sold Itself To TV

If you are under age 35, chances are you have no memory of how much of today's sports programming first got on network TV. They were not always able to pre-empt a Dan Rather evening news program.

To the contrary, 20 years ago, golf, tennis and even professional football were at best secondary TV "filler-fare." It all changed at 7:01 P.M., EST, Sunday, November 17, 1968.

The New York Jets were leading the Oakland Raiders with barely one minute to go. At that moment, 7:00 P.M.—the start of prime time, most of NBC's affiliates were routinely (in hindsight blindly) switched to normal preset evening programming. This evening it was a movie about a little Swiss girl, *Heidi*. Enraged viewers around the country gridlocked station switchboards. Stunned TV executives could not even get through to countermand the blunder. And things got worse the next day when viewers found that the Raiders had come from behind, scoring two touchdowns in less than one minute, to beat the Jets 43-32. Networks and sponsors were scored and scathed for commercially driven arrogance.

The lesson was not lost. Policy for all networks was quickly changed to televise at least pro football games until conclusion. But, to prevent conflicts and hedge loss of sponsor-time advertising, the networks hunkered down on other sports.

Tennis was just struggling to emerge from its country club image to become a spectator sport. Jet travel now permitted better player participation cross country and internationally. Colorful juniors like Jimmy Connors were emerging from the public courts. Minorities like Arthur Ashe were coming up.

But, every effort to get national TV exposure failed. The networks were having none of another "*Heidi* event." Tennis, with its totally unpredictable two-game-lead requirement to win a set, was viewed as particularly unacceptable. The game could, and often did, go on interminably without resolution.

Perhaps in desperation, the tennis fathers had the inspiration to throw this marketing challenge to one of their greatest patrons, Jimmy Van Allen. Jimmy was a noted patrician tennis buff, perceived by some as a maverick. (He was to go on to found the Newport, Rhode Island, Tennis Hall of Fame near his estate there.)

With the challenge of shortening and making game times predictable, he first came up with the short-lived VASS (Van Allen Single Serve . . . cutting time and neutering the Big Serve). But he broke into network time with his original Nine-Point-Tiebreaker, to kick in at six games all. Then service would rotate for no more than nine more points, with the first to reach five winning the set.

Voilà! The networks bought it. Viewers were informed that regular programs would resume only after a match's conclusion, though Van Allen's idea sharply limited that rare necessity. At the Forest Hills U.S. Open, perhaps the first introduction, the colorful Van Allen had a flagpole placed alongside his box so that on a tiebreaker he could run a red flag up it and salute the event. Today, the original Nine-Pointer remains only a boon to social club tennis Round Robins, assuring contestants they will start and finish about the same time without too much cooling off.

Alas.

Once tennis got TV hooked, and the big sponsor money started flowing, its very success was its undoing. The players chickened at so much money riding on a single sudden-death point. Preserving only the six-all feature, they devised and forced the present non-tiebreaker . . . once again requiring a two-point lead for winning a set.

*—February 1990*

# VIEWPOINTS FROM OTHER MAVERICKS

# Sales & Marketing

## Sales A Great Avenue

As a woman who got her start in publishing on the business side, I early on decided that sales was a great avenue, because the proof of one's success was so tangible. As a manager, I've always been hands-on and involved.

*—Cathleen P. Black*
*President*
*Hearst Magazines*

## A Maverick Can (And Better) Produce Results

Bill Gove was a legend as a salesman at 3M. He used to tell this story in motivational talks to the troops.

"I was just starting out in sales when my boss called me in and said, 'Bill, I want you to go to New Orleans and see our field man, Harry. You've never met anyone like him. He's about 60 pounds overweight; his clothes look like a bulletin board for whatever he ate for lunch; he garbles his words, and he writes his orders on the back of a napkin.'

"So I said, 'Sure, I'll go down there. What do you want me to do? Buy him a copy of *Dress For Success?* Put him on a diet? Fire him?'

"'Hell, no. Find out what this guy is eating and make sure he gets all he wants. He's our biggest producer. And while you're down there, you better get some for yourself.'"

That story always worked. Maybe because it was so close to the Abe Lincoln version: "But, Mr. President, Grant drinks!" "Find out what his brand is and send him a case. I need him. He fights."

Could a curmudgeon like Harry or a boozer like Grant be successful today? Of course. You see it all the time in sports. The basketball player who averages 20 points a game is on a longer leash than the backup guard. It isn't fair, and it isn't right, but it's the way of the world in a world where results often matter more than how you get them.

These days, with everything so high-tech, there's less tolerance for the klutz, even a mad demon of a salesperson klutz, because a screw-up on-line can cost the company zillions. Harry's mustard-stained napkins might not pass muster, no matter how big the order.

Earl is the opposite of Harry. He walks around as if he's on his way to run a board meeting. Earl's paperwork is perfect, and his desk is neat. He's on time for every sales meeting, and without having to be begged, he automatically takes a seat in the front row. Earl would be the perfect salesperson except for one thing: He couldn't give away envelopes to Publishers Clearing House. Customers just don't warm up to him.

Most sales people fit somewhere in between Harry and Earl, not daring to be as nonconformist as Harry, but able to avoid setting people's teeth on edge, à la Earl.

Smart companies have come to realize that salespeople need to be rid of duties that have nothing to do with sales. They know that the most productive time salespeople have is the time they spend with their customers, not with their fellow employees. They—and their salespeople—are externally focused. Totally.

Dumb companies remain enmeshed in structure, processes and politics. They tend to be internally focused on the company culture, the company rule book, the company dress code and the company haircut. They have meetings to see if they should have meetings.

Company committees? Internal planning projects? There's Earl in the front row again, his hand raised, volunteering for the job. Earl knows that his future isn't in sales; it's in getting into the bureaucracy. When the Earls of the world get promoted as their reward for doing the grunt work that successful salespeople hate, the regimen of regular sales meetings, new forms to fill out and mandatory attendance take a big leap skyward.

Will Harry's production go up when Earl gets through with him? Of course not, but Harry might make less noise when he eats.

Many of you reading this may work for Earls. Don't toss in the towel. Just keep your own priorities straight. Try not to let Earl waste too much of your time, and just keep shaking and baking.

Mr. October, Reggie Jackson, was not the most beloved guy on the team, but I never heard his managers complain when they were cashing their World Series checks.

**Mackay's Moral:** If you're going to be different, you better produce. Most managers hate mavericks, but all managers love results.

*—Harvey B. Mackay*
*Author*
Swim with the
Sharks

## Selling By Solving Problems

The time is 1957. I am running an advertising agency at 42nd and Broadway, then recognized as the crossroads of the World. It was a totally unglamorous scene. I was heavily into the food industry, especially frozen foods. There were two big brands in the frozen food industry at that time: Birdseye and Seabrook Farms.

N. W. Ayer, one of the oldest and highly respected advertising agencies represented Seabrook for many years. There were strong Philadelphia Mainline ties between the agency and Seabrook management. Seabrook was in trouble. They decided to look for a new advertising agency. Howard Boerner, one of the men who introduced Minute Maid frozen orange juice to America and the world, set up his small frozen food brokerage business. He represented Seabrook in the New York metropolitan market.

Recognizing some of the original work I was doing for other brands in the frozen food category, he set up a meeting for me and Jack Seabrook. Although Jack Seabrook and I came from totally different worlds, we hit it off like ham and eggs. During our meeting, Jack pointed out that his people were talking to many agencies. The decision could take many weeks. He also recognized that I represented the smallest agency in the melange.

Two months passed without a decision. The advertising trade press ran front page and follow-up stories speculating as to which agency would be the winner of the multi-million dollar Seabrook account. It was reported that at least 50 agencies were interviewed. The marketing director, Manning Exton, told me they had pared down the list to 15 agencies. He also indicated that the final decision would be made by one person . . . Jack Seabrook. Manning volunteered that I could call Jack directly, if I wished. I got Jack on the phone immediately.

He told me he was in somewhat of a dilemma. He had seen several impressive agencies and just could not make up his mind. I asked him what he really wanted from an ad agency. When he hesitated, I volunteered: "Isn't it to help you solve many of your serious problems?" He readily agreed. I pointed out that he was now considering one agency out of 15. I told him I could solve 14 problems and let him get on with his business. "How will you do that?" he inquired. I responded: "Appoint me as your advertising agency. You will have eliminated 14 problems." He laughed and agreed. He said: "Leo, you are my advertising agency, but don't tell anyone yet. My advertising manager will call you in ten minutes."

The advertising manager called in ten minutes and told me how hard he fought to have my agency appointed. I thanked him.

*—Leo Greenland*
*CEO*
*Smith/Greenland, Inc.*

## Walking My Stores

"Why me?" was the question I asked myself when John asked me to write about Maverick Managing. "Me—the conventional, orthodox, strait-laced, straight-forward, self-disciplined manager!"

Time passed. Maybe, I hoped, John had forgotten. More time, and then I became embarrassed at not responding to a good friend. Another letter. Another telephone call: "What do you mean, John, by 'maverick?'"

"Well," he replied, "do you remember the time you hired and fired your company's first-ever MBAs—11 in 12 months?" I had forgotten—or at least I didn't want to be reminded.

I remember that in a circle of friends greeting each other for a social occasion, I singled out a college fraternity brother who had achieved since a most outstanding career of practicing orthopedic surgery and who generously gave of his time several weeks each year to the under-privileged children of third-world countries. I spoke nostalgically of his amazing skill of frequently climbing a huge poplar tree that stood in the side yard to the frat house. His response, quietly said, was: "It's amazing what you are remembered for." My career is not to be compared with the good doctor's, but I could not help but think of how it was that after all the places John and I had been and the things we had done together through the years that John would be reminded of me as a Maverick Manager.

I spent most of my time on the road visiting stores. The store manager would meet me at the airport in his car. If the car were clean, I had hopes. If it were dirty and trashy, he would get my management lecture on disciplining oneself to manage and to have the will to manage—starting with getting out of bed early in the morning, shaving, showering, dressing, eating breakfast, and into the car to go to work. If the car were dirty, clean it. If he didn't have the management will to keep his car clean, why am I to expect he would have the will to keep the store clean? The next visit if the car were dirty, I would produce from my briefcase a whisk broom and from my throat a vocal set of instructions on cleaning. On the third visit, it would be "three strikes, you're out," or I would find a clean car and a clean store.

When selling the professional, it's more rewarding if the salesman knows the customer's name and the customer knows the salesman's name. When selling the consumer, it's also rewarding but not as essential. Wearing a name tag is helpful in establishing this relationship from customer to employee. I have lived in the same house and have gone to the same neighborhood barber shop for 45 years. The barbers have never given a world class haircut and at times not even a neighborhood class haircut. The price of the haircut has never been a bargain. Since the first visit, every barber has known my name and I am greeted by name when entering. Do I go there for an ego trip or to get a haircut? I would never admit the former. But also, I have never sought out a place to get either a better haircut or a better price.

Early on, I decided all store employees, for good business reasons, should wear name tags. A small business decision, but one of the most difficult to execute — particularly when it had never been done before and the manager was not thoroughly convinced of its merits. Trying to get several thousand people to do such a simple thing as this was almost the undoing of my management will. Sheer frustration gave birth to new thinking. Instead of "do it," or "do it, please," "do it, because it's good business," "do it, because we will all make more profit sharing"—make it FUN. We will play a game. This is the game: I walk in a store without a name tag. It's fifty dollars to the employee who catches me without; five dollars paid to me for the manger without; and one dollar for any other employee. I lost a few fifty dollars over the years, but it was well worth it.

John, in summation, is this Maverick Managing? Is it street smarts? Is it common sense? It is if it achieves the objective—even firing eleven MBAs after a year of adding nothing to the bottom line.

*—Charles West*
*Founder*
*West Enterprises*

## Fuller Brush . . . With Modifications

After elaborate training, I was assigned a territory and was now out on my own. I was about to learn, though door-to-door selling, if I would have the sticktoitiveness and willingness to accept failure and probably a dozen more dubious and questionable feelings that surface and resurface from this experience. Of course, house-to-house selling presents its first challenge when you must apply all the techniques of body language, conversation and subtle motions and actions that will persuade the lady of the house to let you come in and make a demonstration. When I mention my Fuller Brush experience to someone, they often respond with the comment: "You learned how to put your foot in the door." On the contrary, after the short but positive knock on the door, which hopefully the lady would now open, one would take a step backward. She hopefully would then open the door a little farther.

Let me add here that during my Fuller Brush days, I learned to love cloudy and rainy weather, because my percentage of successful entries into the home went up to almost 100 percent. I presume I had cultivated for myself a new motto: "Love that rain." There were many peddlers ringing doorbells, including the Watkins man who sold vanilla and other cooking extractions. On rainy days I presume people were probably home in bed with the excuse: "I'll get going when the weather is better."

Now, back to our approach at the door where we have not yet gained entry. I had two additional support factors to convince the lady of the house that I expected to come in and make a demonstration. First, I carried an umbrella and always had it in the "up" position when I was at the door. After the first couple of introductory remarks, I closed the umbrella and slipped off my toe rubbers, which was indication number two telling the dear lady that I would not only be dry but my shoes would be dry and clean. This was so effective that I would keep the umbrella and toe rubber technique working even after the rain had let up. I would like to think that I was not falsely representing myself but just pursuing a habit.

*—Don Gabbert*
*Retired CEO*
*Gabbert Furniture*

# PART FIVE

# Investing & Wall Street

## That Hot 'Inside' Market Tip

### If From Friend Or Street 'Pro' Ignore Or Invest Against

Apparently our recent essay, "So You've Got Some Money . . . Now What Do You Do With It?," stirred some juices among our readers. One thing was reaffirmed: By the time we've made it this far we realize we learn more from our mistakes than our successes. Yet, not surprisingly, few of us *(me too!)* want to admit to, much less illustrate for the enlightenment of others, those mistakes.

The column coincided with a dear friend's lament: "Why are we still in drug stocks that are at the moment in apparent congressional disfavor? Sure, they did great for me for a number of years, but . . . why not switch to something cool and growthy, like Microsoft?" *(Hey, guys, anybody else heard that one?)*

My modest essay also appeared concurrently with two major financial management events: the "retirement" of two legendary gurus. Peter Lynch, 53, late of the Magellan Fund; and John *(now Sir John)* Templeton, 80, who sold his Templeton Growth and World Funds.

Although separated by 30 age years, Lynch and Templeton have more in common than the fact that they have two of the best *long-term* track records of any financial managers.

We've never met Lynch. We know him only from his new book and TV talk show appearances. But, as does Templeton, he emphasizes things such as: (1) "Don't trade in-and-out; invest for the longer term. I hold stocks at least three or four years." *(Templeton says their average stock is held for at least five years)*; and (2) "Observant amateurs can find great growth companies in regions and industries they know personally long before the professionals discover them."

We enjoyed Lynch's response to the question if he had any regrets about retiring so young. Lynch: "No way. I compare it to my first hot fudge sundae. Fabulous! Then, the second in succession was, well, good. The third? I almost regurgitated."

### Enter Templeton

My relationship with Templeton goes back 35 years. In 1958 John and his new bride, Irene, were fellow participants with my wife, Kelly, and me at a YPO conference beginning aboard the *S.S. Lurline*, sailing from Long Beach, California and concluding in Hawaii.

Our paths crossed again in the sixties, when he founded Templeton-Damroth and pitched for our then fledgling company profit-sharing trust account. Unfortunately, I let older, seemingly wiser, associates pick another choice on that occasion. It was not until 1979 that the company trust needed a new financial manager and Templeton by that time was out of the advisory business and into mutual funds. I asked John for advice on advisors and he gave me some good ones. But, before we could make the move, Templeton low key advised me that he was starting up a separate Financial Advice division.

Thus, we became their first client, months before the official announcement, heading their new client list, which grew to be festooned with much larger, more prestigious clients.

When I decided to select a buyer for my company in 1988 and "cash-in," it was only natural that I picked for personal financial counsel two firms that I found to be very comfortable with John Templeton's investing principles: Bailard, Biehl & Kaiser and Bessemer Trust.

### Templeton Tip Tidbits

Over years of professional and personal association with John, I was privileged to learn some of his guiding principles.

I pass them on here:

• In order to be right two-thirds of the time, I have to risk being wrong one-third.

• Never follow the crowd.

• The time to sell *may* (you might want to hold) be when the 'smart guys' are buying. The time to buy is when everybody else seems to be selling.

• Keep cool. Don't rush in or out of anything.

• Whether the company is big, small, foreign or domestic, look for bargains only with quality company stocks.

• Diversify your asset investments. No amount of research will outguess unpredictable hurricanes, strikes, or earthquakes.

• An investor who has all the answers doesn't even understand the questions.

• Have faith in the future . . . regardless of swings, even crashes like 1987. With the fall of communism and diminished threat of nuclear war, the U.S. may be about to enter its most glorious period.

In closing the Templeton counsel, I conclude with the Hartman Financial Caveat *(hard-learned)*: "Beware the street-professed financial 'expert,' whether it's a Wall Street arbitrageur, your bridge partner at the country club, or your golfing buddy. Trust yourself. Invest in what you know, not that which you don't."

*—December 1993*

## Pension Fund May Be Your Worst Enemy

That seems a jarring headline, I know. But I was recently shaken up by the observations of our Ocean Reef house guests, highly regarded, conservative and consistent financial manager, Larry Biehl, and his associate, Margaret Kritzer.

Biehl is a managing director of the asset management firm, Bailard, Biehl & Kaiser, and the writer of a monthly investment column in his alumni magazine (Stanford Graduate School of Business). You see him often quoted in *USA Today*, *Wall Street Journal*, etc. I listened.

"The real enemy . . . the basic villain . . . in our debt-dominated business culture of the 80s is the institutional managers who have been gulled into buying increasingly low-grade junk bonds. And you pensioner benefiters in turn put the gun at the institutional managers' heads to manage *'short-term,'* to *'max the immediate results in your portfolio.'"*

All this came up when I lamented about a story that Merrill Lynch (greedily and short-sightedly, I maintain) was trying to outdo the late and unlamented Drexel Burnham Lambert in wooing junk bond investors. Their Presidents Ball (featuring a perhaps gullible Ronald Reagan as a speaker and, of course, Henry Kravis) is a challenge to Drexel's former Beverly Hills social event, the Predators Ball. (Oh, dear, when will they just all slink back into their overpriced condos . . . and leave Real Businesses alone?)

Anyway, my financial gurus have a very big point. As a pensionee, I've got to plead guilty, also, to screwing up our economy as one of those who condone "maximum short-term return-or-you're-fired" yields from our institutional managers. And, maybe, you are too?

Readers cannot be unaware of my long-time low regard for some "Wall Street types"—stockbrokers who churn, arbitrageurs, one-shot deal and fee-driven investment bankers and lawyers.

A new book by *Wall Street Journal* reporters Burrough and Helyar, *Barbarians at the Gate*, describes many of these types as, in effect, the hookers of the business world.

This column has long agreed with LBO financier Ted Forstman (who uses cash only, no junk bonds) that most of the Kravis, Drexel, and other "high risk" paper they create to pay outrageous and unrealistic prices is funny money. And that it is a cancer on real businesses. It's billions of dollars in a new form of the old first-in chain letters—with the institutions then taking in each other's wash to keep the thing going, and not collapsing for lack of new buyers.

Well, all the "smart money" university, insurance, state, county, and union financial managers may have had their last Drexel Predators Ball—and its Merrill Lynch rival party. Meanwhile, Moody's is downgrading Kravis' RJR Nabisco; Campeau's Federated fantasy is over; Kravis has his first big acquisition in Chapter 11; Payments-In-Kind (PIK) bonds (paying more bonds instead of interest due) are being rejected.

Mostly our real businesses, even the more commonsense-leveraged earlier LBOs, are doing well enough.

But as for the more recent deals, both the companies and their parasitic non-real-business lawyers, brokers, investment bankers, the Predator Parties seem all but over.

Just the deck chairs are rearranged.

*—March 1990*

## A Nephew Asks For Investment Advice

*Dear Uncle John:*

*Now that I'm 25 years old, and out in the Real World earning my own money, I currently have most of my savings in a money market bank account. I want to stay kind of conservative, but the problem is that I often find money too available and easy to spend.*

*I would like to put it into a more locked investment. But I'm not too savvy when it comes to money management, IRAs, or any kind of securities. Mom and Dad have offered suggestions, and I wonder if you know of anything I should look into? What do you recommend for a solid portfolio that would mature nicely as I grow older?*

*Sincerely,*
*Your nephew, Matthew Hartman*
*San Francisco, CA*

Dear Matty:

As you probably know I've often written about the four most powerful words in business: "What Do You Think?" That is, it never hurts to ask . . . you might learn something you didn't already know . . . you flatter those you ask . . . you can always just listen and then make up your own mind for your action, if any.

Thus, you got me thinking back 46 years to 1949, when I borrowed $100 from my father *(big money to me in those days!)*. I had just made a sales call on the general manager of the *Toronto Globe & Mail* trying to get him to invest in some advertising space in my magazine, *Sales Management*. W.J.J. Butler said he was sorry there was no budget left for advertising, but, I guess feeling sorry for this tyro space salesman out on his first road trip, said "I'll give you a Canadian Stock Exchange tip, instead.

"Trans Mountain Oil is a new company established to

build a pipeline from the Yukon and British Columbia over the Rockies to mid and Eastern Canada."

Matty, I invested the borrowed $100, reinvested and it doubled and redoubled, paid back the loan, and kept reinvesting. It multiplied into several thousand dollars. Every now and then I'd take a little out, as, for instance, $100 to buy an old Model A Ford to use as a station car to the Darien commuter train.

A problem, answering your question, is that was the only time I invested in a tip. During a long career in contact with many businessmen, I was often inevitably exposed to what might be called legal inside information. I never followed through personally. And while some of their companies did well, at least as often I noted even CEOs exercising stock options found their expectations were not rewarded. So, no tips, I'm sorry.

There was one other kind of an exception where I very early invested in Warren Buffet's Berkshire Hathaway holding company, which is really more like a mutual fund. More on those shortly. Meanwhile, when I have invested, I often remember the advice of my friend John Templeton, perhaps the most successful professional investor over the past 25 years: "In order to be right two-thirds of the time, you have to risk being wrong one-third." And I stick to the things in areas where I know something from personal experience and contact.

But first an admission that at various times I too, just as you, have also not felt "stock market savvy." One reason is that it saddens me to say that Wall Street, the brokerage business, and investment practices continue to change substantially . . . and often not for the better, in my opinion. As time went on, I gradually changed from being a Wall Street worshiper to mildly concerned and then a mistrust of today's Street "conventional wisdoms." And Wall Street more often became a gambling casino, subordinating its primary original mission of providing capital to a free enterprise society.

## Charles Merrill's Lost Legacy

Among brokers today, regrettably, there remain only a rare few houses and individuals who put you, the customer, first and suborn their firm's pressures and special incentives to sell their Flavor of the Month *(which may not be the best Flavor available)*. The original Merrill Lynch (Pierce, Fenner) had a great slogan they widely advertised: "Invest in America!" And they seemed to mean "invest," not gamble, trade, churn, highly leverage as seems the practice today. Donald Regan led the big changes at Merrill Lynch, before leaving to serve as Ronald Reagan's chief of staff *(fortunately, not for long)*.

As for bonds, I feel they are for buying and selling by those who perceive themselves as "professionals;" they are not for holding, by me.

You have to be careful investing with brokers. They are now short-term quarterly profit-oriented as never before. And they may encourage you to leverage with margin *(borrowing from the brokerage)*. I should caution that almost never do sophisticated business executives use margin accounts; generally, according to brokers, only those that can least afford it do so. Margin requirements should be raised to at least 75 percent and maybe one of these days reformers, like Securities and Exchange Chairman Arthur Levitt, will be able to get it through.

Warren Buffet says that trading in exotic futures, options and derivatives should be banished and relegated to the foreign exchanges. So do I, Matty. Stay away from them. I do.

In recent history the banks with their ups and downs have also not generally been good places to seek investment advice. There are perhaps several reasons: Except at the very top, the caliber of bank executives is not comparable to industry, even the separate investment-banking industry. And the bank personnel turnover is relatively high; finding continuity is difficult.

Brokerage/analyst language is too often euphemistic at best; deceitful at worst. "Correction" is the term for falling prices. And "distribution" means they are unloading stock to stock dabblers. And their touting of the cyclicals (automotive, technology, pharmaceuticals) can be hedged endlessly.

**Money Managers and Mutual Funds**

You are absolutely right in looking for investment where it is not too easily accessible to your whims. I'm assuming that at your age your bundle is less that $300,000, which is the minimum you would need to attract a reliable investment management firm. So that leaves mutual funds.

A word of caution on mutual funds. I would avoid those that are listed in the *Wall Street Journal* as the top performers *this year.* The reason: rarely, if ever, do you find the same funds every year. Rather, you should look at those that have established a respectable rate of return for *at least* ten years. The Templeton funds are an example. And don't be put off by funds that charge an initial modest sales fee. The "load" or "no-load" fee is generally insignificant to the fund's value.

At your age, Matty, you can afford to be considerably less conservative in your investments than will be true as you age. Later "preservation of capital" will become more important. *(Of course, the legendary investor Benjamin Graham wisely noted "return of capital" is first priority).* But, for now, even if you take a hit or stagnate, you have many years to recoup.

Finally, I think you should consult with your bank about establishing an IRA. And, most importantly, you should arrange with your bank or mutual fund to have an A.I.P., Automatic Investment Plan, in which each month you have a set amount automatically switched from your incoming funds to the mutual fund for investment.

Hope you find this helpful. Fond regards.

Uncle John

*—October 1995*

## Some Of The Smartest Deals Are Those You Fail To Make

Well, at least we're here. Residing at Ocean Reef is hardly Slumsville. Upon reflection, to make it possible, we've had to do a few things, make a few decisions that were better than the times when they were not so good.

By definition that again brings up the old "batting average" subject. In baseball one out of three makes for a "good" hitter. In the real world it usually takes more like two out of three.

Let me reflect upon a few experiences to make the point. Just over 33 years ago I made a good decision to join the Young Presidents' Organization on a restful cruise to Hawaii aboard the *S.S. Lurline*. I made a bad decision, awaiting castoff from the Long Beach dock, that I wasn't however going to get at all involved with the YPO members *(I thought I was too busy and, mistakenly it turned out, feared they had no interests in common with me. My decision was to be proved immature and underinformed)*.

Only a couple of days out at sea I started a series of better decisions. Among them was my wife meeting the then honeymooning new member, John Templeton and his bride, Irene. His name was later to become famous as perhaps the premier value-investment fund manager over a period of 20-plus years.

About 15 years ago Templeton articulated one of his key philosophies: "In order for me to be a successful investor two-thirds of the time, I have to risk being wrong one-third of the time." The Batting Average.

Then there is the old saw about the merry-go-round and how you have to grab all the brass rings as they go by. Well, yes and no. You actually can improve the Batting Average by *not* grabbing at everything. As I reflect upon my mistakes *(perhaps as with Templeton's one-third)*, most have been a result of two things:

One, making decisions or moves that were primarily tax-driven, i.e., rationalizing purchase or continuation of flawed operations because such was a contribution to overhead, etc.

The second has been being rushed into the conventional-wisdom-of-the-moment: the Flavor of the Month, the trend, the fad, the "in" movements.

Fortunately I never showed much ability or perspicacity to grab onto these latest buzzwords in the bar car of the New Haven RR. When it was "in," I was among those reluctant to "go public" . . . and it turned out later we were much better for it. I was usually last in our industry to get acquisition-happy, preferring natural growth . . . and, again it turned out to be the best course.

We were flatteringly wooed by some of the "in" financial conglomerates of the time, including American Can and Harold Geneen's ITT. Fortunately, I was too dense to comprehend their alleged "synergies." Today, American Can has been gobbled up, ITT is being unbundled, "conglomerates" and "synergy" have become pejorative terms.

I've been lucky. But a challenge remains. How do you tell in advance which are the right two-thirds decisions . . . and which are the bummer one-thirds?

*—September 1995*

# PART SIX

# Trends

## Beware The Conventional Consensus On Trends

In other chapters we have noted that successful unconventional managers respect and take note of "conventional wisdoms" by the "experts." But they don't necessarily abide by them. In fact, by definition, our Unconventional Managers march to a different drummer.

Take my own case, for example. It's been 47 years since the end of World War II and my discharge from the U.S. Navy. My business life since has been in some aspect of sales, marketing, advertising and newspaper/magazine publishing. All these fields are literally awash in "experts." Each succeeding year of experience has sharpened my distrust of "conventional wisdoms." Especially when the experts all agree.

This stance has caused me to be called (by friends) an incorrigible contrarian.

But, contrarianism can imply negativism. In reality, the opposite applies. I've always been an inveterate optimist: An enthusiast, glass-is-half-full, an advocate, but only up to the point at which the "experts" predicting (you name it) cross the majority line in agreeing on the (you name its) future trend.

Instead, to me, history usually demonstrates that the end trend result is certain not to be what a majority consensus predicts. Granted, the experts may have been right at the moment of consensus, based upon the data they thought they had to work with. But, for example, in marketing, there's often a large lag from the time of gross sales results to a later analysis of the real source of those sales.

More importantly, American consumers in particular almost always shift their interests and attention in swings of excess (see golf and tennis equipment examples below).

Action results only after the situation reaches a crisis stage. And a kind of crisis occurs when a majority of experts finally attracts sufficient attention that, in turn, results in action by a majority of the public. But, different than predicted. Maybe more, maybe less—rarely the same as foretold.

### Marketing Non-Trends

Read along with me some examples. In advertising and marketing only a few years ago the "hottest trend setting" advertising agencies, experts agreed, were Britain headquartered Saatchi & Saatchi and Martin Sorrell's clone, WPP. The trendiest thing about both was their "new look of the future:" (1) One-world marketing and (2) One-Stop-One-Shop, offering for clients under one roof a smorgasbord of related and unrelated consulting services, acquired in waves.

It didn't make sense to me. Nor did it to any of my advertising-background golf and tennis partners that I queried. Indeed, I worried that their negativism could be an "expert's consensus" to bet against. Balancing against that, the ad trade press figured these newcomers had a hot hand, and the unfriendly takeover approaches of Sorrell made good current copy. Sadly, and very costly for them, some of our investor friends totally misread the questioning as "just being anti-British."

Today the concept of a One-World-One-Copy-One-Shop is increasingly rejected. Even more so in Europe, where none of yesterday's experts planned or predicted today's peaceful revolution and new marketing realities whereby provincial nationalistic tastes have been vastly sharpened, not homogenized.

As for One-Stop services, Saatchi and Sorrell are now looking for ways to break out and divest their recently acquired consultant services. Meanwhile, these hot-trend agencies of the immediate past are trying to cope with overwhelming debt from their acquisition binges. Coupled with advertising volume falloff, it is little wonder their stock prices have tumbled.

**Futureless Trends**

Remember some of those post World War II predictions in 1946 about what we'd be doing today, 46 years later? Surely by 1992 we'd all have backyard helicopters. Our autos would have long since switched from archaic rubber tires to ride instead on air cushions or along superhighway rails. The rest of our transportation surely would be entirely "mass."

Fueling us, "in 1948, the August *New York Times* promised readers a chemical revolution—producing gasoline from coal—guaranteeing freedom from dependence on foreign oil." (Daniel Yergin, *The Prize*, Simon & Schuster).

Moving on, both our "flower children" and the campus riots were contrary to experts' predictions. The sexual revolutionists foresaw a lot of things, but not AIDS. A sure bet in marketing was that General Motors, with 60 percent of world auto share, would have to be broken up by the government. Ironically, in the spirit of Free Enterprise, GM disdained government intervention. It acted on its own to reduce its market share. Well, maybe more accurately, the folks at GM listened too hard to trend experts who said, "Honda will never be more than a motorcycle shop" and "the Japanese can't handle quality, they will continue to make only distress-sale merchandise."

Remember the 1959 doomsday Club of Rome reports and all of the "scientific consensus" trend predictions based on extrapolations? They mostly didn't happen. Reason: alerted, people just didn't buy it.

The booby prize for wrong or non-predictions by the experts may well be the oil embargo crisis of 1972. According to the esteemed Conference Board's then as now Senior Economist Al Sommers: "Not one economist's computer model had provided for such an unforeseen, unimagined contingency. None. Not Wharton, MIT, Chase, the

Conference Board. We all had to scrap our models and almost start all over again."

Later we got Michael "Debt Is the Way To Go" Milken. Today many firms find they can't pay the frightened banking world enough to make a loan. Or, the banks just don't have it to loan.

### Shifting Yuppie Trends

Continuing with Yuppie examples, many marketers have been burned by getting aboard this trendy market a little too late. An example is "the so-called Tennis Boom. Suddenly the industry lost 19 million players that never existed" (*Forbes*, December 24, 1990). This article notes that "the same thing has happened in golf. The last quarter sales of golf equipment were off 21 percent in dollar volume."

Two misinterpretations of trends happened in both tennis and golf. First, there were major technological changes resulting in existing players trading for new equipment. In tennis, it went from small wood frame racquets to metal or plastic in larger sizes. With golf, the new Ping club designs and Taylor metal woods overwhelmed the existing market with one-time changes.

A second misread trend resulted from the temporary fadistic adoption of the two sports by Yuppies as the current "in bit." First, they latched onto tennis. At the time, 16 years ago, this scared the golf industry even more. With the departure of the caddy supply—and before the cart's advent—golf's popularity declined.

But golf's turn came. Yuppies took it up. And the new popularity of the cart made it possible for a larger base among women and older players. But, after a while, many new Yuppie advocates found advanced golf and tennis play too complex and time consuming. They took up jogging.

Many shin-splints later, the running fad waned. Walking became de rigueur. Now, aerobics is still on a kick. But even more "in," next on the major trend list, for a while, are the muscle-toning and socially collegial health clubs.

What's next? Enjoy your own thing until the experts take it over with a consensus prediction. Then bet against it.

—*October 1992*

## A Baker's Dozen Of Business Trends That May Have A Future

Besides luck and experience, timing is essential for a sustainable business plan. Most successful unconventional managers develop a sixth sense on when and how to tap into a trend.

More importantly, they are astute judges of the differences between apparent flash-in-the-pan passing trends and those that will have more endurance.

As predictions go, you've probably read with some regularity the 12 "signs" that astrologers offer in the daily newspapers. Herewith, for your perusing pleasure, are 13 signs—a baker's dozen. Hopefully, as prognostications, the following entries will eventually bear more validity than zodiac toutings. We include 13 for luck, because, after all, we are unconventional.

### 1. A New Key Wall Street Barometer of Business Health

Standard & Poor's newly established (June 6, 1991) "Mid-Cap Marketing Index" of the stock prices of 400 medium-sized companies will come to be watched with at least equal regard as the Dow Jones. Reasons: The S & P 500 and DJ are favored primarily by traders (as contrasted with investors) and institutions whose personal financial incentives are geared primarily to short-term results, rarely more than a quarter out.

Additionally, bigger companies will continue their 1980s trend of losing relative share of domestic and export product/service sales markets. But mid-sized companies, much less followed and hampered by in-and-out trader demands, will continue their gains in both areas. It will take a few years for the trading-arbitrage community to get the courage and knowledge to start messing up mid-sized companies. Thus, the Mids' business results will be evaluated by stock investors more on the fundamental soundness of the businesses they are in; and more likely, the Mids will be a truer reflection of the state of the general economy.

**2. Trader vs. Investor Distinctions**

These will at last come to be better articulated by business news headline writers and columnists. (Wishful thinking? Probably, but maybe not.) With increased computer sophistication, it will be possible to "asterisk"—in some way—whether an individual stock is favored by traders or investors.

Definitions: A Trader holds stock for computer mini-seconds or until the next quarter. An Investor stays with the stock for up to ten years or more.

**3. Business Education—Financial**

The domination in the 1980s of those with financial smarts will be more subordinate to new imperatives in both operations and deal-making. Today's almost instant sales and inventory controls (à la checkout counters), in contrast to previous hand-count, Nielsen-like shelf samplings, provide knowledge comprehensible to all executives that heretofore only the green eyeshades could decipher—at their own chosen pace. Skills in operations and deal-making, however, must be taught. B-schools will adjust their faculties and curricula accordingly.

**4. Business Education—Management Behavior**

Top B-schools will soon start making mandatory courses in such as "Management By Walking Around." (The "walking around" targets include customers, prospects, and employees.)

Arbitrary, rigid, tops-down Job Descriptions will be replaced by goal-oriented, mutually arrived at employer/employee pacts that can be adjusted as new opportunities arise.

Real-world business feedback to MBA faculties will reinforce the need for newly minted graduates to be low key and not flaunt the advantages of their specialized educations.

The interrogative "What Do You Think?" has been described as being "The Four Most Important Words In Business" by an increasing number of successful managers. Using this question to get input from the rank and file, from customers, from suppliers, even from competitors, will be correctly perceived as a business/competitive advantage. This contrasts with the traditional "Do As I Say" authoritarian hangover from our assembly-line history. Today, "What Do You Think?" is still viewed as too unconventional. ("Ask questions of employees? Why?" executives say. "I'm the manager.") But, the asking of questions should become de rigueur by 1999.

**5. Business Education—General**

Responding to business demand, B-schools will focus even more on Advanced Executive Education, in contrast to two-year MBA training.

Increasingly, companies will want to "train their own." They will select the B-school faculties and the subjects—for two-day to six-week seminars. In some cases, a corollary objective will be for companies to "de-train" or retrain promising MBA graduates whom they have hired.

**6. Bye-Bye To Publicly Flamboyant CEOs**

Boards of Directors will insist that "CEO cover boys" lower their profiles in the consumer press and tabloids; instead, they will be urged to intensify their internal corporate contributions and leadership.

In the 1980s, it was "in" for CEOs to be on magazine covers and in the gossip columns. The perception problems since of Donald Trump, KKR's Henry Kravis, Citicorp's John Reed, Chrysler's Lee Iacocca, and Mesa's T. Boone Pickens have swung the pendulum the other way. Some analysts have noted that downhill slides started within months of a cover appearance. The 1990s corporate culture will more demand: "If our company is doing well, we don't need any distracting and irrelevant publicity."

By definition, today's increasingly effective Participative Management practices mean the non-deification of the traditional "Boss Role." Heard more and more: "I can't get the job done and also take all the credit for it!"

**7. Excessive Outside Consultant Control Will Diminish**

Consultants will still have a place, but not with the often wild excesses of the 1980s. With debt financing less of a factor, responsibility for Mergers & Acquisitions will move back within the companies.

Deals will be more principal-to-principal. Hired gun lawyers and investment bankers (and their fees!) will revert to supporting roles, rather than riding macho shotgun.

**8. Higher Quality Product And Marketing Standards Will Dominate**

"Total Quality-Zero Defects" will become the norm in production. As for sales/marketing/advertising, the One Stop-One Shop advocacies of such as Saatchi & Saatchi and Martin Sorrell's WPP ad agencies will be rejected by client companies even more.

Especially in Europe, newly "1992 merged" nationalistic countries will in fact have heightened provincialism. Except for a handful of Cokes and Pepsis, more, not less, decentralized marketing advertising approaches will be required to counter resentment by potential customers who won't want to be treated as "1992 Monolithic Markets."

Still, new inventory, financing, facsimile, and computer-link technologies will bring many in-house marketing cost savings, domestically and abroad.

**9. Service Management Will Become Highly Imaginative**

Item: A new Lexus car owner, domiciled in the Keys some 30 miles from the Miami dealer, Lexus of Kendall, had a battery failure. It was on a Saturday, naturally. A call found one of the agency's owners still there. Within a half-hour, a loaner was driven down to his Ocean Reef doorstep, and his new car was returned to the shop after a temporary charge up. The following Monday, a dead battery cell located and cured, his new Lexus was back in his garage.

Previously? Remember the days of hanging on the line waiting for a service appointment—convenient for the dealer, not you. And when you finally got it, the customer was responsible for getting the car to the shop, in person or by tow. Partly as a result of this new service concept, the Ocean Reef resident is on his second Lexus and awaiting the delivery of a new coupe in addition.

**10. Better New Products Will Come To The Market—Faster**

The boom in composites for tennis equipment will transfer to other equipment, and not just sports. The new True-Temper composite golf club shafts replacing a single metal is just one example.

Many things now mechanical will become electronic. Holding many of these new products together—the glue of it all—will be newly developed adhesives. And the time from lab to market will be greatly shortened.

**11. Business Security Will Become A Major Industry**

Computerization and new consumer data bases in sales and purchase practices will multiply even faster. Almost instantaneous computer messaging of how consumers vote with their pocketbooks (e.g., electronic pricing and inventory control) will drive and lead many new marketing tactics.

Problem: This data—highly valuable to competitors—remains easy to purloin by hackers and disgruntled/discharged employees. Computer security systems will thus be hot items. So, too, will systems geared to disaster recovery. With so much of our business data now on discs, a flood or a fire in one location can cripple a national enterprise. Think for a minute about your own bank deposits (this will help you feel the strength of the threat). Some computer industry guidelines show that five consecutive days with a down system can put a company out of business.

As to personnel, even today, security guards constitute a staggering 2.6 percent of the U.S. workforce. Their numbers exceed all of the police officers throughout the country. And, the trend will continue.

**12. Mergers Will Be Less Manic For Marketing And Sales Managers.**

These executives are less likely to be "prematurely retired" in the 1990s. Under the unlamented practices of the 1980s, highly leveraged buyouts had imposed on companies huge immediate debt service needs. As a handy variable, sales-marketing-advertising-research expenses were quick-fix costs that could be slashed to balloon cash flow—giving a paper illusion of greater profits. Then the divisions could be broken up and peddled to the Next Greater Fool.

Sadly, often foolishly, the most variable, easily cut costs are the vulnerable outlays for people, travel, and research—but at a tremendous ultimate cost to the future.

Most acquisitions in the 1990s will return to being strategic—and related. Companies acquired will be held and nurtured, rather than rolled over and resold piecemeal a short while later.

**13. Lagging Trend Indicators. LILO (Last In, Last Out)**

Here's one trend that has been around and will always be there. To cushion your sales lost as a result of being a trend laggard, rest assured there will always be some of your customers/prospects playing catch-up. Bless them. They bought belt-in-the-back sport coats and flared cuff trousers just as they went out (still hanging unworn in the closet). They bought gold at its $828 peak. They bought Cadillacs with tail fins the year General Motors phased them. Shed a tear, but thank LILOs for ballast when we miss a trend.

— *September 1991*

## Is Our World Warming . . . Or Cooling?

We were lucky. At least compared to the states to the north of us. Most of them had to declare a storm emergency.

Here in the Keys, warmed by the Gulf Stream, the temperature dipped only to 49 degrees on March 14, 1993. Miami was 37. Further north in Florida alone the cold killed 42. It snowed in Tallahassee. Interestingly, the Blizzard of '93 started on the same March 13 day as did the legendary Great Blizzard of '88, exactly 105 years ago. This year's temperatures are 0.15 below normal. How many times this season have you had your air conditioner on?

All of this reminded me of an essay on the weather I've had on the back burner. Time to bring it forward.

The state of our weather is a common denominator for all of us at Ocean Reef. We talk about it more than anything else. Will it be too cold or too hot? Too wet or too dry? Too rough or too calm? Or, as often . . . just right.

The weather affects more than any single factor our tennis, golf, boating, house guests and grandchildren.

One result is many businesses have products or services where what happens to the weather, hotter or colder, can mean survival or failure. That's why many companies now subscribe to the relatively new service industry of weather forecasting. Its practitioners are known as Climatologists.

Iben Browning was one of the best known. He died in 1990. It's a shame he couldn't have lived a year longer. He would have seen a vindication of his forecast headlined on the front page of the *Washington Post*, August 14, 1991:

***Volcano's Ash is Cooling Earth***

*The explosion of Mount Pinatubo in the Philippines in June, believed to be the largest volcanic eruption of the century, filled the skies with enough dust to cool the earth far more than any effects of global warming (greenhouse effect) might warm it—at least for a few years—new findings released Tuesday show.*

*The dust particles in a belt 15 miles above the earth reflect incoming sunlight from striking and heating the Earth.*

Browning was a contrarian. He was often at odds with the doomsday darlings of the tabloids *(and sometimes more serious media)*. Particularly NASA scientists, headed by one named Hansen, seem always looking for extra dollars with sky-is-falling predictions alarming the world about the warming greenhouse effect. Browning would have none of it.

"Intellectual rubbish," Browning countered. "Primarily because of increased volcano activity—related to sun spot and tide cycle changes—the world, if anything, is getting colder!"

"The World Is Getting Colder."

Huh? Colder? What about the many other current contentions that we are getting warmer?

Even more startling is Browning's forecast: "By the year 2010 the only citrus grown in the U.S. will be in Hawaii."

*—March 1993*

## More On Warming/Cooling

Joe Friday of the National Weather Service says: "It has been record-breaking cold. But it also has been record-breaking with floods." Asked about possible effects of Global Warming, Friday replies: "More than any place in the world, the weather in the U.S. is always changing the most. Last year's number of hurricanes was the second worst since 1933.

"Global warming? Any effect." All we really know is that the atmosphere keeps changing. But we don't know its effect."

Shortly after our first Iben Browning encounter, the maverick *Forbes* magazine came out with an authoritatively documented Dec. 25, 1989 cover story noting that the world was actually not heating up . . . that the situation was mostly the result of NASA rhetoric to get and keep up funding for their activities.

(It is not generally realized that, while some of Alaska's glaciers are indeed receding, others have been growing.)

Noting there is little disagreement with the sun spot cycles coming into a dominant phase, Browning intermixes that with tidal force cycles also converging. (He notes that tide forces have not only a twice daily cycle, but also ones of eight and 179 years.) "All this combined is creating greater volcanic activity among our 70,000 volcanoes . . . 50,000 of which are under water," claims Browning, adding "3,000 are currently active."

"Sun spots and tidal force long-term cycles are beginning to cause massive new volcanic activity," says Browning. "The dust screening the sun will bring on a new glacier age . . . just as it is now almost the sole cause of acid rain."

Huh?

Glaciers?

Well, what about the "Greenhouse Effect?"

"Intellectual garbage," repeats Browning "Only our 11,400 weather stations in the heated cities and airports are getting warmer; the 270 located in the country are getting colder. Russia's crops are failing, because you can't raise crops on ice. Homestead, Fla. in 1989 had a record 27 degrees. Because it's colder, Arctic oil drilling ability is down from 105 to 65 days."

Acid rain? Browning reports the University of Washington studies record the very same amount of acidity in Pacific Western wind-dominated Seattle as in Quebec City. Sweden has found there is no difference in acidity levels when the wind is blowing "clean" from the North Pole as against from the southern industrial West Germany. Browning adds: "Canadian commercial fish catches find smaller length fish, because of less feed. In the northern hemisphere, our tree lines are receding."

Of course, maybe it will all balance out. Browning's glaciers and the warming Greenhouse Effect will cancel each other . . . meaning more of the same.

*—April 1994*

# VIEWPOINTS FROM OTHER MAVERICKS

## Trends

## Start A Trend: 42 Maverick Ideas

1. Work your way *down* the chain of command.
2. Remember the four most important words in business: What Do You Think.
3. Don't spend too much time with the purchasing agent.
4. Use bottoms-up management.
5. Diversify *from* your biggest customers.
6. Don't give. Instead sell a piece of the rock to employees.
7. Rotate the top jobs.
8. Turn the Table of Organization upside down.
9. Throw out the Table of Organization.
10. Talk to others without seeming aggressive, listen without being defensive.
11. Your fortune is not necessarily with the 500.
12. Never assume anything, jump to conclusion, write a scathing memo, without first talking to the fellow manager who causes your anger.
13. Gear your payroll to the most they can make, not the least you can pay.
14. Have decision-making begin with your Line people, then move up.
15. The best faculty at the Business Schools will be the fellow students, not the instructors.
16. Play down your MBA degree.
17. Don't play the "Wall Street trader" game; look beyond the next quarter.
18. A business executive owes zero to arbitrageurs who hold the company stock for trading—not investment (often for only computer mini-seconds).
19. Get a rep for being a "fix-it man."
20. Drive a sharp steely tack that's lean, tough and mean.
21. Rename your Human Resources Department the People Office.
22. Never trust a consensus of "expert" decisions.

23. Take all "expert" advice with a grain of salt.
24. The five magic needs of success: Be healthy, be smart, work hard, be lucky and be FILO (First In, Last Out).
25. Leave the accounting to the accountants, but do your own trend numbers.
26. Don't let your treasurer make up the budget.
27. Throw our your "Christmas Tree" chain of command.
28. Cut down your corporate staff. Then cut again. And again.
29. Throw out "The Book."
30. Spend lots of time asking questions and observing the end-users of your product/service.
31. Get out of your shoes . . . and into your customers.'
32. Sell your prospect the way he wants to be sold, not the way he doesn't.
33. Find the customer's "hot button" by asking questions, asking questions.
34. Don't waste time (yours and your customers) taking them to lunch. Instead use the time to prepare better, travel to the next call.
35. Drop your "I." Accent the "We."
36. Get out of your office chair. Often.
37. For interviews, pull down the blinds behind your office chair.
38. Manage by walking around.
39. Sell by walking around.
40. Get a rep for having the best ear on the block.
41. Abandon "need to know." Maximize fullest disclosure.
42. Don't worry about your competitors also reading this book. Even if they do, only a few will also be successful mavericks and follow through.

*—Ren McPherson*
*and John Hartman*
*The late McPherson was*
*Chairman & CEO of Dana Corp.*

## Mavericks Sometimes Win

From my long ago bringing-up in Texas, my conception of a maverick is a steer that didn't want to go with the herd to the slaughter. They have long been around the business world as well. During the days, when "diversification" was a popular buzzword, the mavericks used to be the ones who avoided it (like myself).

During the "downsizing," which *naturally* followed diversification, the mavericks seemed to be those who did it carefully and incrementally. The second step now seems to be "outsourcing." Also, during the current mega-merger period, which naturally followed "downsizing," the mavericks seem to be those who still don't go along with "bigger is better."

In today's trend toward further diversity, the mavericks are those who long ago recognized the importance of a prudent policy of encouraging "affirmative action" despite counterproductive laws and regulations.

We are in the middle of a heating-up political battle. Many of the new members of the House and Senate view themselves as mavericks. If they stand up against the herd of "big government" steers, they may be able to keep us all from the slaughter. Sometimes the mavericks win!

*—Maurice "Butch" Granville*
*Retired CEO*
*Texaco Corporation*

# PART SEVEN

# What Makes A Maverick?

## The Case For Being Unconventionally Non-Conforming

Can you be a constructive "maverick?" Is being a maverick the same as being a contrarian? Must you be unconventional all of the time or just some of the time? Does being a non-conformist mean you must be anti-establishment? Can viewing your customers and product unconventionally be effective in business?

Yes, no, just some of the time, no, definitely yes.

Questions like this arose when one of our publishers noted a chapter heading in our earlier book, *Second Thoughts*. It was titled "The Unconventional Manager" and included several essays (some of which appear in this book) such as "Kick Your Best Manager Out Of The Office," "Golden Ground Rules For Unconventional Managers" and "Shortest Distance Between Two Points Is Rarely A Straight Line."

"The idea intrigues us, Hartman. Can you research it further and make it into a full length book? Can you supplement it with successful experiences of other mavericks?" asked the publisher.

This book is an attempt to meet that challenge. It includes many reflections and experiences from successful business maverick leaders. But, first, a brief answer to the questions posed at this article's opening:

Question: Can you be a constructive maverick? Answer: A recently published study of 1,000 mavericks, aged 16 to 92, was just reviewed by Brigid Grauman in the *Wall Street Journal* (*Eccentrics* by David Weeks and Jamie James, Villard). "Most people want to be unique, happy—and popular," says Weeks. "Eccentrics are able to attain all these things, get away with more than most people, through the sheer thrust of their personality."

Question: Is maverick the same as contrarian? Answer:

No, they are really quite different. A contrarian doggedly is an "againster." The maverick, on the other hand, picks his spots. *(Hey readers. I won't go through that "his or hers" nonsense each time. Please, just accept I mean both genders.)* He has a positive plan for non-conformity. One of *Eccentrics* favorite examples is the 19th-century British naturalist (studying the fauna of the Amazonian rain forests) who slept with one bare foot dangling from his hammock in the hope of experiencing being bitten by a vampire bat. (Now that's dedicated maverickness).

Question: Does being unconventional mean you must be anti-establishment? To the contrary. Often the mavericks, working within and alongside, are the catalysts that permit the establishment to survive and grow. The successful unconventionalists are rarely radical extremists. They look for an extra edge—maybe only a five percent difference from the conventional wisdoms—in approaching challenges.

And making a difference is not hitting a home run every five times at bat. More often it's making a lot of singles.

Question: Can viewing your customers and your product unconventionally be effective in business? Absolutely. One characteristic in common to all mavericks is their disdain for "the conventional wisdoms," no matter what the subject. This is more than just a healthy skepticism (not cynicism, which is strictly negative). They have learned, with good reason, that once "the experts" reach a more than 50 percent consensus on whatever, things will just not happen the consensus way. One reason: crisis and extremes move people to do things differently. Until such as a "consensus crisis" people are not that concerned about acting one way or another, much less predictably. When they do, it is always not as predicted by the consensus.

Are mavericks willing to take reasonable risks? Legendary investment manager John Templeton says: "In order to come out right two-thirds of the time, you have to risk being wrong one-third."

And mavericks are also usually good as "participative managers" perhaps because of their non-conventional (and non-threatening) insights perceived as contributions by their colleagues.

**Maverick Traits**

The Weeks-James study includes interesting observations on mavericks. Among them:

Maverick traits: They are non-conforming, creative, strongly curious, idealistic (wanting to make the world a better place and the people in it happier), aware from childhood of being different, intelligent, opinionated, outspoken, convinced of being right, not in need of reassurance, have a mischievous sense of humor.

Historical mavericks: Davy Crockett, Lincoln, Charlie Chaplin, Einstein, Dorothy Parker, Howard Hughes are but some examples.

Maverick roots: Most of *Eccentrics'* examples are American and British, with a heavy dose of Scots. "Eccentricity is universal and eternal. It has been with us since the beginning of time, simply because the minute a norm is established there will always be someone to flout it."

Maverick health: They tend to fall ill less often than the average person, and they tend to be more contented, even if they can drive their own entourage mad. "The intellectual excitement that the eccentric experiences tends to trigger the same growth hormone as sex and exercise, which helps keep people young," according to Weeks.

Maverickness is not schizophrenia: "Schizophrenia involves the dissolution of personality . . . whereas with eccentrics (mavericks) the personality tends to become more pronounced."

Heavy-handed maverickness: *The Wall Street Journal* book review of *Eccentrics* concludes with an example of maverickness being perhaps carried too far. They cite the case of the one whose special technique for keeping strangers out of his railway compartment was to read his newspaper upside down and take his temperature every five minutes.

*—November 1995*

## Are Backward Cap Kids Mavericks?

Can mavericks be mavericks even after everybody else starts wearing their hats backwards?

It depends why the so-called maverick started wearing his hat backwards in the first place. If it was simply to be first, to be different, then no, he was merely a pop trendsetter and he'll have to move on to piercing safety pins through his lips (whoops, that's been done already) or whatever. But, if he broke new ground for a sound reason (say, to keep the hat from blowing off while roller-blading), then his idea will remain maverick even after the habit catches on. As creator of the idea, backward cap kid No. 1 maintains at least partial maverick status. (Sounds like bar logic that would last a couple of rounds, but probably no longer. But hey, they didn't give me a philosophy degree for nothing. Actually, I suspect it was mostly just to get me off campus and out of the Dean's hair for good.)

*—Rick VanGrouw*
*Newspaper Editor*

## Unconventional Photography

My interest in photography dates back to the magical moment at the University of Wisconsin when, under the eerie yellow of the darkroom safelight, a black and white image slowly appeared in a tray of developer.

Then followed years of the rigid rules of the camera club competitions when one-third of the photograph had to be clouds, one-third foreground, one-third primary subject matter that had to be just off center. The more clouds the better; the sharper the image from foreground to infinity the better. There had to be something in the foreground to give depth to the scene, and we would hold up ratty looking branches in front of the camera if there were no trees around.

As the variety and versatility of photographic equipment improved once the Japanese recognized that there was something besides the American 4x5 speed graphic, the two-and-a-quarter format and the fixed lens 35s pioneered by the Germans, my friends in the camera clubs became equipment junkies and had their wives sewing "Nikon" and "Canon" patches on everything they wore, still living with the clouds, the depth of field, and the foreground branches.

This coupled with a plethora of the Christmas cards showing pajamed children with red eyes in front of brick fireplaces (with the mandatory stockings hanging from the mantel) caused me to wonder if there were another direction to the art, and I started taking photographs that not many people understood.

I multiple exposed. I zoomed. I went out of focus and added movement where I could. I distorted color. I got rid of skies and placed my subjects in forbidden locations. For intentional blur, I had the guides herd the animals in Africa. I had my transparencies layered. I did my best to create something that had a perspective, a color, a distortion, a feeling that said to me: "I took this and others wouldn't see it this way" not that that endeared me to many of my viewers, although I liked the feeling.

To put it another way, after showing a series of "neat" things to a mute audience, they came alive with a sunrise in the Himalayas, the most hackneyed shot that I showed that night. Somehow people equate great photography with sunrises and sunsets, to me the easiest and least interesting subjects to shoot.

Today, the reaction is mixed. The way-out things that I do that really satisfy me are generally liked by virtually nobody including my Brooks Institute-trained-daughter. So the things that see the light of day are a mixed bag of fairly conventional shots with as much "jazz" as I dare allow.

I do, however, sell a number of prints, and people like my Christmas cards. So I have an excuse to keep buying film, lugging cameras, striving for the one great shot that will really satisfy me.

The future is bright. I now have everything I need for computer enhancement and manipulation that is really wild, but at the moment a little too avant garde for those around me.

When I look at the art world's photographically acceptable era of broken toilet seats, out-of-focus neon designs, scruffy broken trees, fornicating people, and tattooed prisoners, I'm not sure that someday manipulation, or creativity as I chose to call it, won't be acceptable and photography will be released from the straitjacket of absolute purity. (Purity means: "this is exactly how the scene looked when I took it.")

Even Ansel Adams, the guru of purity, spent days in the darkroom dodging and burning to get the exact effect he wanted. Unfortunately, before the process began he had to lug an 8x10 view camera into the wilderness and wait for days to get the colors and lighting he wanted.

With my lightweight 35mm camera, my bag of lenses and filters and my 125mb computer, I don't have to wait for the light. My only barrier is my ability to see and create.

Much like great jazz, the kick to this ongoing quest is looking at a scene, a person, an object and then creating an image that is somehow greater or more interesting than reality.

*—William Ryan*
*President and CEO*
*Ryan, Inc.*

# INDEX